Liz Curtis Higgs

Loved by God

Trusting His Promises
& Experiencing His Blessings

Leader Guide

SAMPSON RESOURCES
4887 ALPHA, SUITE 220 • DALLAS, TEXAS 75244
(972) 387-2806 • (800) 371-5248 • FAX 972-387-0150
WWW.SAMPSONRESOURCES.COM   INFO@SAMPSONRESOURCES.COM

© 2004 THE SAMPSON COMPANY (ALL RIGHTS RESERVED)

What others are saying about Liz Curtis Higgs and *Loved by God*

"*Loved by God* is a must for every women's ministry!"
Debbie Stuart, Director of Women's Ministry
Prestonwood Baptist Church, Dallas, TX

"What a master storyteller Liz is. She makes the Bible come alive."
Amie Price, Women's Ministries
RiverTree Christian Church, Massillon, OH

"*Loved by God* is an inspiring Bible study. You'll be blessed.
And I love the workbook!"
Melissa Shaver, Director of Women's Ministries
The Heights Baptist Church, Richardson, TX

"I am constantly amazed at Liz's biblical depth, understanding, and the tremendous way she shares it. Truly, she has been anointed of God."
Evelyn Blount, Executive Director
South Carolina Women's Missionary Union

"*Loved by God* will touch your heart and encourage your spirit."
Kay Daigle, Women's Ministry Director
Northwest Bible Church, Dallas, TX

"Liz was a hit with our audience! She is a gift to my life!"
Gloria Gaither, Praise Gathering, Indianapolis, IN

"We have laughed and cried and been encouraged that God loves us."
Debra Lavin, President, Alliance Women
First Alliance Church, Erie, PA

"Liz is a true master at touching the hearts of people. She's fantastic!"
Judy Russell, wife of Bob Russell, Senior Minister
Southeast Christian Church, Louisville, KY

CONTENTS

A Note from Liz Curtis Higgs

elcome to *Loved by God,* a six-week, in-depth Bible study designed especially for my sisters in Christ! Together, you and I will help women learn how to embrace God's unconditional love, trust God's wonderful promises, and accept God's count-less blessings, even on those days when we feel we don't deserve them.

God gave us his holy Word—the Bible—to teach us who he is and how we are to respond to him. Your heartfelt commitment to lead this study is a big step, but have no fear—you are *not* alone. Just as others will be praying for you, I will carry you in my heart as well, grateful to have you partnering with me in this unique learning opportunity. I know God will use you to touch the lives of women by leading them, praying for them, and learning with them.

As I wrote this study, thinking about the women who will walk through your door, I kept three goals in mind: that they will discover how much God loves them; that they will realize they can trust God's promises; and that they will experi-ence God's blessings in an eye-opening, life-changing way. Anything you can do to help accomplish these goals will serve your women well.

This Leader Guide has been created to help you plan, promote, and direct the study of *Loved by God.* On the following pages you will find detailed information on the four parts of this Bible study, suggested meeting formats, thoughts on plan-ning and promotion, leadership guidelines, tips for small group leaders, simple ways to encourage women to study God's Word, and prayer recommendations. May God guide you through the weeks to come!

Liz Curtis Higgs

A Four-Part Bible Study

There are four elements to this Bible study: personal study, group discussion, principles and applications, and video sessions. All parts are equally important. Let's look at them.

Personal Study: The purpose of the workbook is to give participants an organized way to spend time with God daily as they read the Scriptures and answer the questions for that day. Encourage the women to find a specific time each day for study and to follow the five-day schedule. This plan will help them absorb the material in small increments rather than being overwhelmed at the end of the week. It also helps participants reflect throughout the week on what they're learning. Many women may be participating in a Bible study for the first time. Assure them of the value of a disciplined study time, and recommend that they answer the questions themselves, using the Bible as their primary source, rather than ask others for their opinions. This way the answers are more personal, more scriptural, and therefore more meaningful. Even if a woman is stumped by a question, she can look forward to the group discussion time when she'll hear others' perspectives and no doubt discover she isn't the only one who struggles at times to answer a question.

Group Discussion: The group discussion period will be a vital weekly feature of the study. Depending on the number of participants, this may require dividing into several smaller groups. It is suggested that there be no more than twelve in a group. Women will be encouraged to share their workbook answers from their daily study time, creating a sense of Christian fellowship, bonding, and accountability within the group. They'll look forward to hearing one another's responses to specific questions, which will help give them perspective on the subject as well as enhance their understanding of Scripture.

Principles and Applications: For Bible study to become a heart-changing, life-transforming experience, we must *identify* the principles at work and *apply* them to our personal situations. Therefore, a key part of each week's class is a time to discuss principles and applications so that women are encouraged to move from *studying* God's Word to *applying* it daily.

Principles are timeless truths found in Scripture—simple, straightforward truths that can be applied to our lives today. Some of the women in your group may be new at studying God's Word, so you will need to guide them through this process. Encourage women not to *read into* the Scriptures but instead to *pull out* truth from the verses they are studying.

Application means putting into practice the principles found in Scripture. When we help women move forward from principles to application, the value of Bible study increases exponentially.

To help women transition from ancient story to modern lifestyle, you will find in this Leader Guide one principle and one application that can be drawn from each lesson. Encourage the class to discuss other possible principles and applications they gleaned from the study, and share your own insights as well. People will suggest different applications because of their unique circumstances, which will expand the group's awareness of God's relevance in our daily lives.

Some of your attendees will have studied God's Word for many years and will move through principles and applications quickly. For those women, your challenge will be to teach them to discover fresh truths in familiar material. Urge them to look for new applications. Since these women may be at different stages in their lives since the last time they studied this story, they will have new eyes to see old truths. As you lead them through this part of the discussion, you may want to

frequently remind them to apply these truths to experiences that have occurred in the last few months. We don't want to live in the past; rather, we want to apply Scripture in ever-new ways that address our current circumstances.

Video Sessions: Each session on DVD is thirty minutes long. The women will gain new insights as they listen to the weekly teaching from Genesis, covered verse by verse—a teaching enhanced by extensive biblical research and personal experience. The women will participate during the video session through careful listening, by taking notes in the space allotted in their workbooks, and also by laughing. All three methods—listening, note taking, and laughing—contribute to the learning process. Hearing the Scripture presented in this way will help women remember the verses they've studied as well as the lessons they've learned.

Suggested Meeting Formats

Loved by God is a flexible Bible study for women, suitable for various time frames and environments. Three possible meeting formats follow that allow for different settings—church, classroom, or home—and one to two hours designated for the study. Some women enjoy a time of fellowship with snacks and drinks before the meeting begins. Others who are concerned with busy schedules may prefer to get directly into the study. Pray about the format that best suits the women who will be involved.

Whatever schedule you follow, allow time for the women to move from one element to the next—opening, discussion, video—and keep announcements and distractions to a minimum.

If childcare is offered, be sure to schedule drop-off *prior* to the official starting time for the Bible study. Regardless, make sure the women understand that class will begin promptly at the time designated…then start on time!

One-Hour Bible Study Format

10 minutes:	**Group Participation**—Have prayer requests written out by participants in advance so requests can be handled succinctly.
15 minutes:	**Discussion Time**—Review only the questions that require explanation or have strong, biblical concepts that need to be emphasized. Discuss at least one principle from the week and its possible applications. Encourage the women to make notes in the "After Your Group Discussion…" box in their workbooks.
30 minutes:	**Video**—Watch the video together.
5 minutes:	**Closing Prayer/Encouragement for the Week**—Send them off with a prayer and a promise of what is to come.

Ninety-Minute Bible Study Format (recommended)

10 minutes:	**Large Group Participation**—Welcome everyone and open with a prayer. Consider spending a short time in worship to prepare hearts.
30 minutes:	**Small Group Discussion**—Review the workbook questions and discuss the primary principles and applications from the week's lessons. Allow a few minutes at the end of this time for participants to fill in the "After Your Group Discussion…" boxes.
10 minutes:	**Small Group Prayer Time**—Spend a few minutes praying for each other's needs.
30 minutes:	**Video**—Gather everyone to watch the video.

10 minutes: **Closing Prayer/Encouragement for the Week**—Bring a sense of closure to the class time and give a brief preview of the next lesson. Include points from the video in your prayer. Encourage them to do their personal study daily.

Two-Hour Bible Study Format

10 minutes: **Fellowship/Refreshments**
10 minutes: **Large Group Participation**
40 minutes: **Small Group Discussion**
15 minutes: **Small Group Prayer Time**
 5 minutes: **Short Break**
30 minutes: **Video**
10 minutes: **Closing Prayer/Encouragement for the Week**

Planning and Promotion

Once you have chosen the day, time, and format for the seven weeks of your Bible study, detailed preparation can begin. Here are some important points to consider:

♦ **Budget**—Meet with a staff representative and learn the goals of the church regarding this study as a resource to area women. If the church sees this as an outreach ministry and has sufficient funds in the budget, you may want to provide workbooks at no cost or set up a supplemental fund to reduce the price of the workbooks for participants.

♦ **Room Reservation**—If you have chosen to meet at the church building, work with the facilities coordinator to have a room reserved on a weekly basis for the event. Agree on the room layout so that it looks the same each week. The arrangement of tables and chairs depends on the size of your study. Here are two suggestions for room setup: (1) Place round tables with eight chairs each throughout the room. Every table represents a small group. Have the women sit at their designated table each week. This can become their place for small group discussion as well as prayer time. The women can turn their chairs for viewing the video. (2) Organize the space in classroom style with rectangular tables and chairs. The women can sit at the tables for the opening and then move their chairs into smaller circles for the discussion period. Or they can all be together for discussion time and move to smaller, intimate circles for prayer time.

♦ **Childcare coordination**—If childcare will be offered, you'll need to work with your preschool minister or the person responsible for that department to schedule babysitters and to ensure that all insurance concerns are addressed. If you will be meeting in a private home, you may want to arrange for an older teenager to watch the children. Or schedule rotations of two women each week to watch the children during the discussion and video times.

♦ **Promotion**—Good promotion is necessary for a successful Bible study. Women won't know about this exciting opportunity unless you tell them! Place posters around the church describing the study, time, location, price, and childcare registration information. The kit includes various promotional items for use in your church bulletin or newsletter. In addition, the graphics files and promotional copy are included on audio CD #4 in a folder/directory for use on your computer. Simply insert the CD into the CD drive of your computer and open the directory of the CD. A folder/directory will appear on the screen with promotional materials inside, which you can copy and paste into your own documents.

♦ **Registration**—Set up a table at a convenient spot for women to register after they attend church services or Bible classes. Have leaders available to answer questions about the study. Early registration is important so you can evaluate the needs of your group, determine how many small group leaders will be needed, create those small groups, and pray for those who have registered. Small group dynamics work best with eight to twelve women per group. On your registration list, request all the information you might need: name, age, occupation, telephone number, e-mail address, and childcare needs. This will allow you to prepare in advance for group size and childcare requirements.

♦ **Nametags**—People enjoy knowing the name of those they meet! Prepare nametags in advance for those who have registered. A JPEG file is included on the promotional CD (audio CD #4) that you can use in your word processor to create your own nametags, or you can use prepackaged nametags if you prefer. Have temporary blank nametags at the first session for women who come without having registered in advance. Make sure everyone feels welcome!

♦ **TV/DVD equipment**—Reserve all equipment needed for the seven weeks (Introduction plus six weeks of study), and make certain the equipment is set up and working an hour or more before the meeting starts.

Leadership Guidelines

Depending on the size of the Bible study group and the location of your weekly meetings, various leaders will be needed to make the study successful and enjoyable for everyone. If you have a group of sixteen women or more, you will need to form small groups for discussion. This will create an intimate setting, allow more women to share their workbook answers, and be less intimidating for the quieter participants. For the sake of this guide, we will assume the numbers are higher than sixteen women. Feel free to adjust the following guidelines based on the needs of your group.

Director—She is the liaison to the church staff and should be strong in all aspects of leadership. She has the gift of administration and is good at making decisions on the spot and resolving problems. She may have led Bible studies in the past and already be familiar with the many details that must be managed. She is prepared to motivate her team and works well with different personalities, helping everyone accept and enjoy each other. The director will need to prayerfully consider and recruit the rest of the leaders long before the introductory session. Prayer is essential in that process. Even though a person is gifted as a leader, she might be going through a stressful time and not be ready to lead others at the moment. Remember, the director and the small group leaders don't need to be Bible teachers, but they do need to be good facilitators.

Small Group Leader—This person is strong in her faith, growing in her relationship with the Lord, and nurturing and compassionate to other women. She has a heart for encouraging women to grow in Christ. A good small group leader prays for her women daily, prepares her questions in advance, and prayerfully considers which questions will be best to discuss each session. She has the ability to move the women smoothly from question to question and makes everyone feel comfortable, whether they are new to the Bible or have studied God's Word for years. A skilled small group leader will manage the process so that everyone participates, including the quieter ones. An effective small group leader is willing to contact people individually and prays with them when a need arises.

Secretary—This detail-oriented woman ensures the workbooks have been ordered and made available and takes care of the introductory meeting particulars: nametags, workbook sales, and getting the A-V equipment in place and working. She may want to keep an updated list of attendees. She may also call or e-mail women each week to encourage them.

Refreshment/Fellowship Coordinator—This person loves any social event! She coordinates the weekly refreshments with the women. If a closing celebration dinner or fellowship time before or after the final session is planned, she will coordinate everything for that event.

Twelve Tips for Small Group Leaders

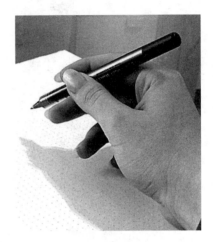

1. To capture everyone's attention from the very start, consider using a visual aid, a meaningful poem, a surprising statistic, a relevant news story, a pithy question, or anything else that will illustrate the Genesis narrative and engage the women's interest. You'll also find here a suggested Welcome Warmup for each week's lesson. Feel free to be creative and come up with something else that suits your own style and your group's needs.

2. Small groups quickly develop a "prayer personality": chattier groups like to pray for the needs of individuals who are present, while studious groups prefer sticking to a brief prayer for the session and plunging into the workbook questions. You will set the tone for the weeks to follow. Consider carefully how much time you want to allow each week for prayer and how comfortable your group will be with sharing such needs. Short and to the point is the best way to begin; otherwise this sharing time can easily take over the study time!

3. Relax in knowing that your primary role is to facilitate the discussion of what the women have learned in their private Bible study time the previous week. You don't need to have the answers to all the questions that might arise. Your job is to keep things on track, biblically and practically, and to make your group session upbeat and productive for everyone.

4. Good listening skills—smiling, nodding, maintaining eye contact—communicate to each woman that her words matter and her involvement is appreciated. Such validation is one of the most important things a facilitator can do. Call each group member by name and make her feel welcome with everything you say and do.

5. Create a nonthreatening atmosphere for discussion. Instead of correcting or criticizing—even nonverbally with a wrinkled brow or slight frown—focus on helping women find the most biblically sound answers to their questions. Keep things positive. Say "Yes, and…" rather than "No, but…" If someone gets long-winded, gently summarize her comments and move on. If someone rambles or seems confused, clarify her comments as best you can and get back on track. In either case, thank her for contributing.

6. Encourage the quieter class members to participate without putting them on the spot. If they are looking at you, they are probably prepared to share. If they have their heads down or their eyes averted, wait for another question. Try to balance the participation so that a few people don't dominate the discussion each week. Your more reticent members will appreciate it.

7. Keep the discussion directed toward the Bible and personal application so comments don't stray into nonproductive speculation. Human opinions are interesting, but biblical truth is *life changing!* After all, the goal of Bible study is to learn more about the Bible, not more about each other, delightful as that is. Keeping God's Word at the center of your discussion time will bear much fruit.

8. Please review the video lesson on DVD or CD each week *before* your group meets. That way you can steer your class discussion away from material you know will be covered, avoiding redundancy. Plus you can prepare their hearts for the message to follow.

9. Resist the temptation to do most of the talking. Rather than sharing what *you* have discovered, urge others to share what *they* have discovered. Offer your comments after other women have offered theirs and only if your answer enhances, rather than repeats, what has already been said. This takes discipline…but you can do it, sis!

10. Encourage participants to raise questions that came up during the week. If you don't have the answer, promise to do further study and come back the next week with additional insights. One of the real joys of facilitating is gleaning new truths about God's Word from solid commentaries and research books and from people who are farther along in their spiritual growth.

11. Engender enthusiasm for the next week's lesson with a "teaser" about what's to come. You'll find a bit of that at the end of each video. See if you, too, can find something in the next lesson that will pique the women's interest and keep them coming back.

12. Check out one or more of the fifteen resources suggested at the end of the workbook to further your understanding of the passages in this Bible study. The ones listed are a good starting point, but many excellent commentaries are available, especially on the book of Genesis. If your church doesn't have a library, your pastor might let you peruse his study shelves. Or visit your local Christian bookstore and make some good investments in your own spiritual growth.

Eight Simple Ways to Encourage Women to Study the Bible

Our hearts' desire is to see women's lives changed by the timeless truths of Scripture. Here are some easy points to share—in your own words if you prefer—to convince your attendees that daily Bible study is truly worth the time and effort.

1. *You can handle it!* This study centers on a relatively small portion of Scripture, so each day's Bible study can be done in twenty to thirty minutes.

2. *Take it easy on yourself!* Do one lesson each day rather than doing all five days at once. That way God Word's can penetrate your heart and be reinforced daily.

3. *Love those stories!* We're studying a portion of Scripture that is entirely narrative, and don't we all enjoy a good story? Even those of us who think we know this tale will come to see these people and events in a new way.

4. *You're not alone!* When you study the Bible, you're in good company. The Holy Spirit moves in your heart, teaching you, guiding you, and empowering you.

5. *Make it special!* Select a pleasant spot to study each day, a place as free from distraction as possible. Let your family know this is *your* time with God.

6. *Write it on your heart!* Memorize key verses or write them out and place them in a prominent place as a way to instill God's principles in your heart and mind.

7. *Check it out!* In addition to using your favorite Bible, check out other translations as well. Web sites can change quickly, but http://bible.gospelcom.net is a good one, providing access to at least seventeen versions, including the New International Version, the New American Standard Bible, the Amplified Bible, the New King James Version, and more contemporary Bibles such as The Message and the New Living Translation.

8. *Give God room!* Remember that God's Word is "living and active. Sharper than any double-edged sword, it penetrates even to dividing soul and spirit, joints and marrow; it judges the thoughts and attitudes of the heart" (Hebrews 4:12). If you want to grow, you have to give God access to your heart and let his Word do its mighty work.

Prayer Recommendations

Prayer is by far the most important part of any Bible study. As soon as you decide to lead this study, begin to pray for every aspect, including the promotion, the registration, the technical details, even the atmosphere of the weekly meetings. Above all, pray for women's hearts to be open to learning more about God and applying his truth to their lives as they begin to grow in his wisdom.

If you are a director, pray for your leaders, specifically that they will guide their women toward God's truth and that there will be no complications during the weekly study times. Pray that God will use you to encourage your leaders and to teach them new ways to help others.

If you are a small group leader, pray for the women in your group and let them know you pray for them regularly. Pray that the women will bond as a group and discover they can depend on each other. Pray for the time in your small group to go smoothly. Pray that hard-to-understand questions will be answered in a way that brings contentment, not contention. Pray for discernment in knowing which questions to review each week and which principles and applications will be the most effective. For any questions that might require additional explanation, pray that you will address each one without fear or concern. God is the Leader of your group. Trust him to guide you.

Weekly Session Format

Your Bible study may involve hundreds of women and dozens of small groups, or it may be a circle of friends sitting around a living room. It may be confined to one hour or extend to two hours or more. Whatever your style or circumstances, here is a detailed checklist you might want to follow each week.

Preparation

♦ Pray for each woman throughout the week.
♦ Have the Welcome Warmup copied onto cards or slips of paper for the women to receive as they come in.
♦ Touch base with the members of your team (church administrator, small group leaders, secretary, refreshment coordinator) by telephone, e-mail, or a face-to-face meeting to make sure their responsibilities have been fulfilled and they are ready for the Bible study.
♦ Make certain the tables, chairs, and equipment will be available and set up in advance.
♦ Arrive early to prepare yourself and pray for the week's study.

Opening

♦ Have the women pick up the Welcome Warmup card as they come in, and encourage them to take a moment to read the card and prepare their thoughts as the rest of the class arrives.
♦ Welcome everyone and open with a prayer.
♦ Consider spending a short time in worship to help women turn their hearts toward God.

Welcome Warmup

WELCOME WARMUP
Share a time when you didn't receive the discipline you deserve instead, you received mercy from another individual.

♦ Open the discussion time with the Welcome Warmup exercise or some other activity you have created to lead into the week's lessons.

Group Discussion

♦ Determine in advance which questions from the week's lesson are the *most* critical to cover in the discussion period, and make sure to address those. Generally these will not be questions involving the basics of the biblical story, which are thoroughly covered in the video. Instead choose those questions that were more difficult to answer or required more personal introspection. Encourage the women to answer *all* the questions during the week, even though not all will be covered in your group time.
♦ After you've discussed your selected questions, ask the group for any other questions they'd like to cover before moving on to principles and application.
♦ As you have opportunity, reinforce the three goals mentioned in the introductory video:
  1. To know how much God loves us
  2. To realize we can trust his promises—as long as we don't insist God meet our timetables
  3. To experience God's blessings—as long as we are willing to look at a new definition of "blessing"

Principle and Application

♦ The Leader Guide outlines the steps for each week's lesson and suggests a principle and application for each day of the study. After prayerful consideration, select one or two principles from the week, as well as the corresponding applications, to share and discuss with your group.

♦ Taking this next step—applying the truths of God's Word to our lives—truly opens eyes and hearts, encouraging women to move up another level in their study time with God.

♦ Encourage the class to discuss other principles and applications they may have gleaned from the study, and share your own insights as well.

♦ Allow a few minutes at the end of this time for participants to fill in the "After Your Group Discussion…" boxes in their workbooks before starting the video.

Video

♦ Encourage the women as they watch to jot down in their Video Notes section the points that are especially meaningful to them. You may want to make your notes when you preview the video.

♦ Gather and watch the video as a group.

Closing Prayer/Encouragement for the Week

♦ Briefly share your favorite point from the video to encourage the women as you bring the class to a close for the week.

♦ Assure them that your time together has been a blessing for you and that you hope they've gained from it as well.

♦ Let them know what they will be studying in the week ahead.

♦ Close the meeting with a prayer. You may want to use something from the video as a prayer focus.

Now that you have a description of the weekly elements, in the following pages you'll find specific guidelines for each of the seven weeks, including the daily principles and applications. May God bless you richly as you lead women toward an amazing truth: they are *loved by God!*

Welcome to the Family!

God's Plans for Us Are Bigger Than We Can Imagine

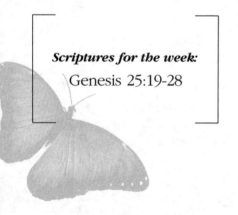

Scriptures for the week:
Genesis 25:19-28

OPENING

♦ Welcome the women.
♦ Introduce yourself and tell them of your excitement and anticipation for the Bible study.
♦ There are many clever ways to begin bonding the women. Come up with a brief icebreaker that will liven the room with laughter.
♦ Allow the women to introduce themselves and quickly tell something about their lives (maybe who lives in their home, how long they've lived in the area, or their favorite pastime). Whatever the size of your group, keep this time short.
♦ Introduce other leaders for the Bible study.

EXPECTATIONS OF THE BIBLE STUDY

♦ Describe the four parts of the study.
♦ Outline the format for the study and how each weekly session will flow. Make sure participants understand that you will begin on time each week.
♦ Explain the Welcome Warmup.
♦ Encourage everyone to complete the workbook questions each week so the discussion time will be meaningful and productive.
♦ Assure them that their personal study time will take no more than twenty to thirty minutes each day. Of course, the more they put into the study, the more they will be blessed!

VIDEO

♦ Watch the video as a group.

CLOSING PRAYER/ENCOURAGEMENT FOR THE WEEK

♦ Tell them that over the next week they'll be studying the actions and motives of some well-known characters from the Old Testament. They will soon see that, despite our behavior, God honors his promises.

Sibling Rivalry

God Honors His Promises, Even When We Don't

CHECKLIST

❏ Preparation completed

❏ Welcome Warmups copied

WELCOME WARMUP

As the women come in, give them this statement printed on a card: *Share a time when you didn't receive the discipline you deserved; instead, you received mercy from another individual.*

OPENING

Begin on time. Welcome the women and open in prayer. As you pray, include elements in the prayer that will bring to mind the past week's lesson as well as point ahead to the principles and applications that will be discussed later in the session. This will help women leave behind any outside distractions and prepare their hearts to focus on the Bible study and the lessons God has for them.

GROUP DISCUSSION

Warmup: Ask the members of your group to share a time in which they didn't receive the discipline they deserved but were the recipients of someone's mercy instead. (If necessary, share an example from your own life to get the discussion started.)

After listening to the women's comments, remind everyone to incorporate what they've learned about undeserved mercy into their discussion of the week's questions by making this point: *Grace is a gift, not a reward for good behavior. Mercy is extended because of God's divine nature and faithfulness and despite our human nature and lack of faithfulness.*

Discussion: Have attendees open to their prepared answers for this week's lesson. Cover the most important questions. Because of time constraints, choose only one or two principles and applications from the following list to discuss with the group. In the final minutes of your discussion time, ask the women to complete the "After Your Group Discussion…" box in their workbooks and then share their responses with the group as time permits.

Scriptures for the week:
Genesis 25:27-34;
26:34-35; 27:1-29

Principles and Applications

Day One: A Bold Bargain

Principle:

♦ Fleshly desires cannot compare to developing an appetite for the things of God.

Application:

♦ As you think through the last few days, what rash decisions did you make based on a momentary need or "hunger"—whether for food, control, pleasure, material goods, love, attention, etc.? Were your choices in line with Scripture? How did those decisions affect you? When we allow an immediate human need or desire to overshadow the long-term spiritual consequences, we can make costly mistakes.

Day Two: Older but Not Wiser

Principle:

♦ God's blessings are not to be devalued or taken for granted.

Application:

♦ How has God blessed you today? If you were aware of the blessing at the time, how did you thank him? We need to be alert to God's blessings in our lives and continually praise him for his generosity.

Day Three: An Aging Father, a Scheming Mother

Principle:

♦ Our best sources of wise counsel are God's Word and God's people.

Application:

♦ As you think about your week, what advice have you taken from another person? Is he or she a child of God? Does that person want the best for you…or for himself or herself? Take into consideration whom you are taking advice from, learn from your mistakes, and next time seek wise, godly counsel.

Day Four: A Hairy Plan

Principle:

♦ God hates any lie, any deception of others or of ourselves.

Application:

♦ Review your last few days. What have you thought, said, or done that you wish you could take back? As Christians, our speech and our actions should reflect what is good and right and true so we don't bring reproach on ourselves or on God.

Day Five: Blessings for the Deceiver

Principle:

♦ We can trust God to honor his promises, just as he honored his promise to bless Abraham, Isaac, and Jacob.

Application:

♦ Is there something in your past that keeps you from trusting others or even from trusting God fully and completely? Just as God was faithful to honor his promises to these patriarchs, we can trust every promise he has made to us in his Word.

VIDEO

Gather and watch the video as a group.

CLOSING PRAYER/ENCOURAGEMENT FOR THE WEEK

Bring a sense of closure to the class time and point to the next lesson, letting everyone know that in the week ahead they'll be studying certain human behaviors and learning more about God's faithfulness. End with prayer.

Running from God

God Knows All About Prodigal Children

CHECKLIST

❏ Preparation completed

❏ Welcome Warmups copied

WELCOME WARMUP

As the women come in, give them this statement printed on a card: *Think of an example of a prodigal you know. Using discretion, briefly share that person's story.*

OPENING

Begin on time. Welcome the women and open in prayer. As you pray, include elements in the prayer that will bring to mind the past week's lesson as well as point ahead to the principles and applications that will be discussed later in the session. This will help women leave behind any outside distractions and prepare their hearts to focus on the Bible study and the lessons God has for them.

GROUP DISCUSSION

Warmup: Ask people to think of an example of a prodigal they know. Have two or three briefly recount their stories, and then discuss why the testimony of a prodigal may sometimes be more powerful than the testimony of a person who has never turned away from God.

After listening to the women's comments, remind everyone to incorporate what they've learned about prodigals into their discussion of the week's questions by making this point: *You will hear two additional powerful stories of prodigals in today's video.*

Discussion: Have attendees open to their prepared answers for this week's lesson. Cover the most important questions. Because of time constraints, choose only one or two principles and applications from the following list to discuss with the group. In the final minutes of your discussion time, ask the women to complete the "After Your Group Discussion…" box in their workbooks and then share their responses with the group as time permits.

> **Scriptures for the week:**
> Genesis 27:30–28:9

Principles and Applications

Day One: A Matter of Minutes

Principle:
- We must always be aware of our choices and behavior. How we respond to situations can affect the rest of our lives.

Application:
- Have you ever been manipulated into doing something you did not want to do? How did you initially respond to the situation? Looking back, how might you have handled things differently? Even if we have been treated badly, venting our anger only harms us further. A good antidote for anger is remembering God's faithfulness and mercy toward us, even when we deserved *his* anger.

Day Two: Bitter Tears

Principle:
- The consequences of our actions are often unavoidable.

Application:
- What consequences are you living with today because of a selfish action or rash decision in your past? Because God is gracious and full of mercy, we should seriously consider the changes we need to make in our lives—personally, relationally, and especially spiritually—and then take action, rather than continuing to make wrong choices. As children of God, we have the power to start fresh and begin to make godly decisions.

Day Three: Out for Revenge

Principle:
- No matter the situation, it is not our job, but God's, to take revenge.

Application:
- Share an incident where you responded to an unjust situation without seeking godly counsel through prayer or advice from another Christian. Did you try to settle the score? If so, how did you feel afterward? We must release our desire to get even and instead trust God to handle things. If anger and revenge have become habits in our lives, we should look below the surface to determine why.

Day Four: A Family Split

Principle:
- God's promises to his people will be fulfilled no matter how desperate the situation may appear at the moment.

Application:
- Has some aspect of your life wounded you so deeply that you consider yourself unworthy of love? Perhaps you are a victim of abuse, divorce, or alcoholism and still bear the scars. Maybe you have created your own unhappy situation from selfish choices that now affect the people you care about most—a spouse, child, parent, or friend. We may believe we have failed so miserably that God could never forgive or love us again. Yet God has promised his children that he will love them no matter what, that he will forgive them continually, and that he will restore their hearts and cleanse their spirits.

Day Five: Misguided Steps

Principle:

♦ Decisions based on resentment, jealousy, or revenge are not honoring to God and will only make matters worse.

Application:

♦ Make a list of emotions that you have on a daily or weekly basis. Categorize them, noting which emotions are sinful and selfish and which are good and godly. Think of an emotion you expressed recently. Was your response selfish or godly? As we make decisions and plans for our lives, we should measure them against the wisdom of God's Word rather than base them on our changeable emotional states.

VIDEO

Gather and watch the video as a group.

CLOSING PRAYER/ENCOURAGEMENT FOR THE WEEK

Bring a sense of closure to the class time and point to the next lesson, letting everyone know they will see a turn in the story next week as they sense God's presence and begin to understand how much he truly loves his people. End with prayer.

Loved by God

A Dream Come True

God's Love Knows No Bounds

Scriptures for the week:
Genesis 28:10-22

CHECKLIST

❑ Preparation completed

❑ Empty chair with "God" sign in place

❑ Welcome Warmups copied

WELCOME WARMUP

As the women come in, give them this statement printed on a card: *As you enter, notice God's chair in the room and acknowledge his presence in some meaningful way.*

OPENING

Begin on time. Welcome the women and open in prayer. As you pray, include elements in the prayer that will bring to mind the past week's lesson as well as point ahead to the principles and applications that will be discussed later in the session. This will help women leave behind any outside distractions and prepare their hearts to focus on the Bible study and the lessons God has for them.

GROUP DISCUSSION

Warmup: You will have already placed a chair in the room and put a sign on it that says "God." At the beginning of the class, explain that they are to act as though God is sitting in that chair, listening to their discussion. Throughout the discussion, continue to remind them of his holy presence as you discuss "God with us."

Notice the mood of the room. Is it quieter than in weeks past? Are nicer words being spoken? Have the women explain any changes from the normal mood of the room. After listening to the women's comments, remind everyone to incorporate what they've learned about God's holy presence into their discussion of the week's questions by making this point: *Although God's chair is at the front of the room, he can hear your conversations in your small group, too, and can discern the thoughts and intentions of your heart.*

Discussion: Have attendees open to their prepared answers for this week's lesson. Cover the most important questions. Because of time constraints, choose only one or two principles and applications from the following list to discuss with the group. In the final minutes of your discussion time, ask the women to complete the "After Your Group Discussion…" box in their workbooks and then share their responses with the group as time permits.

Principles and Applications

Day One: Divine Communication

Principle:

♦ God comes to help those who are unworthy of his help.

Application:

♦ What have you done in your life that you don't think God will ever overlook? Is it a damaging lie, an affair, abusive behavior, or an illegal action? God takes us as we are. Jacob did not "deserve" God's help, and yet God extended it. In the same way, although we are undeserving of God's attention, God loves us "as is." Indeed, "God is our refuge and strength, an ever-present help in trouble" (Psalm 46:1).

Day Two: God's Promise and Presence

Principle:

♦ When God speaks, it is with authority, and we know that he has spoken.

Application:

♦ Has there been an instance in your life when you knew God "spoke" to you? Maybe it was during your prayer time, or maybe he communicated to you through a friend, spouse, or parent. Share your experience with the group. If you cannot give an example of this in your life, perhaps it's a matter of perception. You may have credited someone or something else for a word of wisdom that came from on high. God desires to communicate with each of us, and he does this through his Word, through prayer, and through fellowship with other believers. Become aware of the truth that God wants to have a relationship with you, and begin to listen for the ways he is speaking to you.

Day Three: Sacred Sites

Principle:

♦ The "fear of the Lord"—giving him the reverence, respect, and honor due him—brings life.

Application:

♦ What words would you use to describe your view of God? How has your perception of him changed over the years? We are not to be afraid of God, seeing him as angry and judgmental and watching to catch us in a mistake so he can punish us. Instead, we are to be in awe of a perfectly holy God who loves his highly imperfect people.

Day Four: More Than a Name Change

Principle:

♦ The most important decision we can ever make is to commit to the Lord that he will be our God.

Application:

♦ Have you committed your life to the Lord? If so, will you share that publicly during this time of discussion? That commitment changes everything in our lives—what we say, what we do, how we spend our time, how we treat other people, and ultimately where we will spend eternity.

Day Five: Jacob's Promises and Offerings

Principle:

♦ God gives to us so that we can give back to him. Our attitude should be right so that we give freely and cheerfully.

Application:

♦ What gift has God given you that you might use to bless others? Maybe it's a financial gift, a musical talent, the ability to teach, or simply the desire to serve. Periodically look at the gifts and blessings God has given you, and determine if you're purposefully giving back your time, money, and talents to God.

VIDEO

Gather and watch the video as a group.

CLOSING PRAYER/ENCOURAGEMENT FOR THE WEEK

Bring a sense of closure to the class time and point to the next lesson, explaining that next week they will consider the difference between our "inside" selves and our "outside" selves and will discuss what commitment means. End with prayer.

Blinded by Love

Man Looks at the Outward Appearance; God Looks at the Heart

CHECKLIST

❏ Preparation completed

❏ Welcome Warmups copied

WELCOME WARMUP

As the women come in, give them this statement printed on a card: *Silently choose someone in the room and quickly write down the first three things you notice about that person. Next, write down three important qualities any person should have.*

OPENING

Begin on time. Welcome the women and open in prayer. As you pray, include elements in the prayer that will bring to mind the past week's lesson as well as point ahead to the principles and applications that will be discussed later in the session. This will help women leave behind any outside distractions and prepare their hearts to focus on the Bible study and the lessons God has for them.

GROUP DISCUSSION

Warmup: Make sure everyone had time to jot down quickly the first three things they *noticed* about the person they selected and what they consider to be the three most important *qualities* of a person. If a chalkboard or whiteboard is available, make a list of their top choice in both categories. If no board is available, simply have the women share their lists.

After listening to the women's comments, remind everyone to incorporate what they've learned about inward and outward attributes into their discussion of the week's questions by making this point: *Although we focus on our external qualities, God looks at our internal qualities. Think about how you can change your viewpoint to be more like God's.*

Discussion: Have attendees open to their prepared answers for this week's lesson. Cover the most important questions. Because of time constraints, choose only one or two principles and applications from the following list to discuss with the group. In the final minutes of your discussion time, ask the women to complete the "After Your Group Discussion…" box in their workbooks and then share their responses with the group as time permits.

Scriptures for the week:
Genesis 29:1-20

Principles and Applications

Day One: Journey's End

Principle:
♦ When we become a child of God, our character changes to become more like him, but the transformation is a lifetime process.

Application:
♦ What characteristics about yourself do you see changing as you draw closer to God? Some people may notice drastic changes while others detect more subtle shifts in attitude and behavior, yet God sees them all, big and small.

Day Two: Jacob Meets His Love

Principle:
♦ God will give us strength and purpose when we are committed to him.

Application:
♦ What is happening in your life right now that requires God's strength to endure? If you will commit your situation to him, he will give you the strength you need.

Day Three: Jacob Meets His Match

Principle:
♦ We should be quick to listen and slow to speak, choosing our words carefully.

Application:
♦ What decision have you made this week without considering all the aspects involved? What could be the consequences? Most of us are slow to listen and quick to speak! If we would simply follow God's order—quick to listen, slow to speak—we might avoid future heartache.

Day Four: Beauty Seen and Unseen

Principle:
♦ The outward beauty of others may steer us in the wrong direction.

Application:
♦ When you walk into a roomful of strangers, are you drawn to people who look successful or say the right things in a meeting or have material possessions you would like to own? Maybe you reach out to others who look like you, or perhaps you seek friendships with women who are quite the opposite of you. As we learn to care more about our appearance to God and less about our appearance to others, we will become more "beautiful" on the inside, and our outward appearance will be transformed as well. In the same manner, we should accept people the way God created them to be and not make shallow judgments based on appearance.

Day Five: The Price of Love

Principle:

♦ Once you make a commitment, do everything possible to fulfill your obligation.

Application:

♦ Think of a commitment you have made recently—a work project, a promise to a child, or an agreement to pray for a friend. Have you kept your commitment? It's important to act with integrity. When you vow to do something, big or small, think of it as a commitment to God himself and keep your commitment to the end.

VIDEO

Gather and watch the video as a group.

CLOSING PRAYER/ENCOURAGEMENT FOR THE WEEK

Bring a sense of closure to the class time and point to the next lesson, telling everyone to expect the unexpected in next week's portion of the biblical story as we watch God's discipline at work in Jacob's life and in ours. End with prayer.

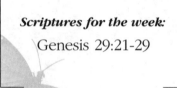

A Deceiver Deceived

God Disciplines the Ones He Loves

> *Scriptures for the week:*
> Genesis 29:21-29

CHECKLIST

❏ Preparation completed

❏ Welcome Warmups copied

WELCOME WARMUP

As the women come in, give them this statement printed on a card: *What rules would you recommend for disciplining an adult in a work situation who has violated a company policy?*

OPENING

Begin on time. Welcome the women and open in prayer. As you pray, include elements in the prayer that will bring to mind the past week's lesson as well as point ahead to the principles and applications that will be discussed later in the session. This will help women leave behind any outside distractions and prepare their hearts to focus on the Bible study and the lessons God has for them.

GROUP DISCUSSION

Warmup: Using a chalkboard, whiteboard, poster board, or large tablet, ask the class to give you their "rules" for disciplining adults in a work situation. Then compare that list to the one God might generate if he were explaining why he disciplines us. Follow up with a discussion of the nature and value of God's discipline.

After writing both kinds of discipline on the board—human and divine—encourage your women to think about this exercise as they go into their discussion time by emphasizing this point: *Consider why it is important to know and understand God's discipline.*

Discussion: Have attendees open to their prepared answers for this week's lesson. Cover the most important questions. Because of time constraints, choose only one or two principles and applications from the following list to discuss with the group. In the final minutes of your discussion time, ask the women to complete the "After Your Group Discussion…" box in their workbooks and then share their responses with the group as time permits.

Principles and Applications

Day One: A Big Switch

Principle:

♦ Following God doesn't insulate a person from mistreatment and sorrow.

Application:

♦ Have you suffered through a recent ordeal that caught you by surprise, even though you were honestly doing everything right? When we find ourselves in difficult circumstances, the question to ask is not "Where is God in this?" or "Why did God let this happen?" but "How can God use me in this situation for a good purpose?"

Days Two: Vixen or Victim?

Principle:

♦ We are responsible to God for our actions.

Application:

♦ Think of an unfortunate incident in your life that never should have happened. Were you the instigator or the victim? Is there anything you can do now to make it right? Perhaps you need to pray for forgiveness for your actions or forgiveness for your bitterness resulting from the situation. Nothing is accomplished by blaming others.

Day Three: Just Deserts?

Principle:

♦ As sinners, we deserve to die—"For the wages of sin is death." But God saves us through his gift of grace—"the gift of God is eternal life in Christ Jesus our Lord" (Romans 6:23).

Application:

♦ Do you find yourself pointing out the sins of others rather than recognizing your own sins? Instead of expending our energy ensuring that others get what they "deserve," we should be grateful for the great mercy we have received from God and extend that mercy to others.

Day Four: A Rude Awakening

Principle:

♦ Although our anger may be directed toward another person, our underlying anger is often aimed at God.

Application:

♦ Recall an event in your life that you thought was unfair. What emotional baggage do you still bear from that situation, and why are you still carrying it? What can you do to begin to recover from this situation—to heal, to forgive, and to move on? Whether we feel angry, bitter, sad, or lonely, those emotions can interfere with our relationship with God if we find ourselves blaming him for our disappointment. To strengthen our relationship with God, we must deal with our emotions and allow him to heal us.

Day Five: A Second Wife

Principle:

♦ We reap what we sow. "The one who sows to please his sinful nature, from that nature will reap destruction" (Galatians 6:8).

Application:

♦ Are there areas in your thought life that have begun to spiral out of control? Although no one can see our thoughts, they *can* see the results since our thoughts control our words and actions. It's easy to see that Jacob reaped the heartache he sowed. It's harder to face those results in our own lives. We must take these sins as seriously as God does, realizing the great consequences they have on others and on our spiritual lives.

VIDEO

Gather and watch the video as a group.

CLOSING PRAYER/ENCOURAGEMENT FOR THE WEEK

Bring a sense of closure to the class time and point to the next lesson, reminding the group that they have only one week left in this Bible study, the most important week of all, which demonstrates the power of God's love and how it can change our hearts and lives for eternity. Encourage them not to miss next week—we've saved the best for last! Then end with prayer.

A Heart for God

God's Love Is Powerful Enough to Change Our Hearts

CHECKLIST

❏ Preparation completed

❏ Welcome Warmups copied

WELCOME WARMUP

As the women come in, give them this statement printed on a card: *Write out your own words of praise to God, thanking him for something good that has happened to you through this study. If you have a favorite psalm, share that as well.*

OPENING

Begin on time. Welcome the women and open in prayer. As you pray, include elements in the prayer that will bring to mind the past week's lesson as well as point ahead to the principles and applications that will be discussed later in the session. This will help women leave behind any outside distractions and prepare their hearts to focus on the Bible study and the lessons God has for them.

GROUP DISCUSSION

Warmup: Taking your cue from Leah, begin with an extended time of praise to God. Ask several class members to share their written praises or read a few verses from their favorite psalm. Sing a praise song together, or ask several people to add their brief thoughts to an opening prayer of praise.

After your time of worship, remind everyone to incorporate what they've learned about praising God into their discussion of the week's questions by making this point: *There were three goals for this Bible study. Praise God for any and all of these changes he has made in your life.*

1. *Have you come to realize how much God loves you?*
2. *Have you learned to trust his promises…and his timing?*
3. *Have you experienced God's blessings…and redefined "blessing"?*

Discussion: Have attendees open to their prepared answers for this week's lesson. Cover the most important questions. Because of time constraints, choose only one or two principles and applications from the following list to discuss with the group. In the final minutes of your discussion time, ask the women to complete the "After Your Group Discussion…" box in their workbooks and then share their responses with the group as time permits.

> **Scriptures for the week:**
> Genesis 29:30-35

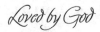

Principles and Applications

Day One: Room for Two?

Principle:
- What man considers "manipulation," God may call "discipline," using the situation to mold us into the image of his Son.

Application:
- Is there a situation in your life—a close relationship, a job, a friendship—that's hard for you to handle and often doesn't seem fair? What have you learned from that situation? When we go through hardships, God will use them for our ultimate good and for the purpose of drawing us closer to him.

Day Two: Precious in God's Sight

Principle:
- God sees us, values us, loves us, and comforts us.

Application:
- Have you been through a difficult trial where you felt completely alone, abandoned, even unloved? Perhaps the death of a parent, the loss of a child, or a painful divorce? What a comfort to know we are *not* alone. God sees our circumstances and responds in love.

Day Three: Blessings for the Humble

Principle:
- "God opposes the proud but gives grace to the humble" (James 4:6) and meets their deepest needs.

Application:
- When does God reveal himself most to you—in prosperity or adversity? In easy circumstances or difficult ones? As we see God at work in our lives, we can begin relinquishing our will to God's, giving him the glory for whatever happens rather than taking credit ourselves.

Day Four: The One Who Always Hears

Principle:
- God blesses us in order to demonstrate his character.

Application:
- In what ways have you been blessed this week—whether a visible blessing or the silent blessing of being still and knowing that he is God? Did you deserve the blessings you received? What did you learn about God during those times of blessing? We don't have to earn God's love or do anything to receive his blessing.

Day Five: Praise the Lord

Principle:

♦ God deserves our full and complete praise.

Application:

♦ How has your day been? Your week? Can you praise God for every hour, even if some of them didn't go as you had hoped? As we grow in our knowledge of God—who he is and what he has done for us—our hearts fill with love and our lips with gratitude and praise.

VIDEO

Gather and watch the video as a group.

CLOSING PRAYER/ENCOURAGEMENT FOR THE WEEK

Bring a sense of closure to the class time and to this study. Thank the women for participating faithfully each week, and encourage them to continue to think about what they have learned and to stay in God's Word daily. Assure them that they truly are "loved by God"…and so, dear leader, are you! Then end with prayer.

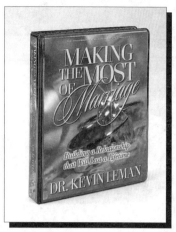

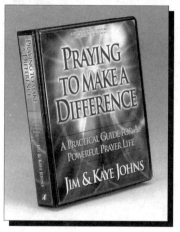

Liz Curtis Higgs

Loved by God

Trusting His Promises
& Experiencing His Blessings

A Bible Study Workbook

SAMPSON RESOURCES

CONTENTS

Welcome to the Family!

God's Plans for Us Are Bigger Than We Can Imagine

GENESIS 25:19-28

Welcome to the Family!

 h, dear sister, what a thrilling journey awaits us!

I am honored to lead the way as we study the lives of Jacob and Esau, Leah and Rachel and discover what it truly means to be loved by God. If you've ever doubted God's love for you or felt unworthy of his blessings, you've come to the right place.

We'll soon learn that Jacob used every trick in the book to achieve success on his own terms before his past caught up with him…and still God stood by him: "Yet I have loved Jacob" (Malachi 1:2). Leah, meanwhile, tried her best to earn Jacob's undivided devotion, yet received God's unconditional love instead when he blessed her with children: "When the LORD saw that Leah was not loved, he opened her womb…" (Genesis 29:31).

What a heart-changing difference this story has made in my own walk with God! Imagine what God will do in your life as you open his timeless Word and watch it come alive.

Do yourself a favor and complete your lessons each day—I promise it won't take very long—using whatever Bible you most enjoy. My primary translation is the New International Version (NIV). I'd encourage you to locate other translations in your favorite bookstore or online to enhance your understanding of each passage.

There are optional questions, marked with a ♥ that will add to your growth and understanding. Wise is the woman who finds a few extra minutes to explore those questions…and *forgiven* is the woman whose busy life won't allow that additional study just now. At the end of each day's lesson appears a prayer, which I've intentionally left open-ended. Please take a moment to add your own heartfelt words for our loving, listening God to hear.

In your small-group time, share the principles you've learned and the ways they apply to your daily life. After all, the truths found in the Bible are meant not only to be studied but also to be put into action. Women at various stages of spiritual growth will be seated around you. Why not encourage the "younger" women and draw strength from those who have known God's love longer so that it becomes a meaningful time for every participant?

Come walk with me, friend, as we embark on a journey together that will change your life forever!

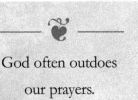

God often outdoes

our prayers.

MATTHEW HENRY

God's Plans for Us Are Bigger Than We Can Imagine

Today's lesson: Genesis 25:19-28

Major events:

- Jacob and Esau are born to Isaac and Rebekah after many struggles.

- Each parent chooses a favorite, pitting the brothers against each other.

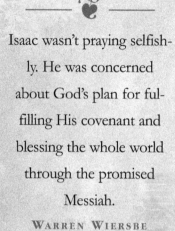

Isaac wasn't praying selfishly. He was concerned about God's plan for fulfilling His covenant and blessing the whole world through the promised Messiah.

WARREN WIERSBE

Video Notes

Sibling Rivalry

God Honors His Promises, Even When We Don't

Sibling Rivalry

God Honors His Promises, Even When We Don't

Read Genesis 25:27-34; 26:34-35; 27:1-29.

Major events:

■ Esau sells his birthright to Jacob for a bowl of stew and later marries poorly.

■ Rebekah disguises Jacob, who proceeds to steal Esau's blessing.

■ Isaac unintentionally blesses his younger son, Jacob.

This week's verse to remember:
"God is no mere human! He doesn't tell lies or change his mind. God always keeps his promises." (Numbers 23:19, CEV)

 his week we'll find out what sort of young men these two brothers became, shaped and molded as they were by their older parents, each of whom picked a favorite son. Dangerous practice, that. Had the boys been identical twins, we might have seen more similarities, not only in their looks, but in their personalities and preferences as well. Instead, they become as different as night and day, as dark and light, as hairy and smooth.

Jacob had more than smooth skin, though; he had a smooth way of handling his brother to get what he wanted. A manipulative parent may (unintentionally) teach a child the value of persuasive speech and clever finagling.

You'll soon see that the drama in these scenes is of a domestic nature. Not big, parting-of-the-Red-Sea stuff. Just family gatherings around a meal. But gatherings marked by deception. Three centuries before the birth of Christ, Demosthenes wrote, "Nothing is more easy than to deceive one's self." Deception and self-deception are at the heart of this week's lesson.

When we study the family of Isaac and Rebekah, we may shake our heads and say, "Dysfunctional with a capital *D!*" Rebekah and Jacob fell into the traps of self-deception and rationalization, dragging Isaac and Esau along for a bumpy ride and permanently changing all their lives in the process. And if we're not careful, we can do the same.

Day One: A Bold Bargain

Read Genesis 25:27-28.

1. Both Rebekah and Isaac were on hand to raise their sons, yet it seems they did not parent in the same fashion. Whom did each parent favor and why?

_____

_____

2. If you've seen parental favoritism in a family, how did that preferential treatment affect the child's...

relationship with the other parent?

_____

_____

relationship(s) with his or her sibling(s)?

_____

_____

relationship with God (if apparent)?

_____

_____

> They personified two ways of life typical for Palestine, which at that time was more wooded: that of the hunter and that of the shepherd.
>
> GERHARD VON RAD

3. If you have children, do you relate to them in the same ways? Even if you have twins, do you find yourself relating to one better than the other?

_____

How can you understand one child better than another and yet not show favoritism?

_____

_____

While we wouldn't condone favoritism, what does a parent do when a child has special needs, is chronically ill, or has suffered a trauma? How can you give special attention to one child, when necessary, without favoring that child?

_____

_____

_____

4. What do the following verses teach us about our responsibilities as parents—or as anyone who has influence over the lives of children?

Deuteronomy 5:29 _____

Deuteronomy 11:18-21 _____

Ephesians 6:4 _____

Read Genesis 25:29-34.

5. In this short but dramatic scene, what trade does Jacob suggest, and why is it audacious?

_____

_____

6. The birthright "applied to certain advantages, privileges, and responsibilities of firstborn baby boys....The *advantages* and privileges were that this baby became the object of special affection and would legally receive a double portion of his father's estate. The *responsibilities* were that he was expected to assume the spiritual leadership of the family. He was also required to provide food, clothing, and other necessities for his mother until her death and all unmarried sisters until their marriage." To better understand the cultural significance of this role, look up these other instances of the "firstborn." What does each tell us about the significance of the firstborn?

Deuteronomy 15:19 _____

Deuteronomy 21:15-17 _____

Luke 2:23 _____

Hebrews 1:6 (To whom is this specifically referring?) _____

Revelation 1:5 _____

7. Let's look first at Jacob's role in this exchange. A matter of mere seconds separated his birth from Esau's, yet in that culture those seconds would make all the difference in what he inherited and his role in the family. How might Jacob have justified bargaining with Esau for the birthright?

_____

_____

Do you think he wanted the earthly blessings, or do you think he was aware of God's promise to his mother and he was just "helping God" fulfill the promise? Why do you think this? Refer to Genesis 25:19-28.

_____

_____

8. Although the concept of the blessings of birthright may seem foreign to you, have you ever been in a work situation where someone else got the promotion, the raise, the perks, or the praise even though you were just as deserving? Which of the following best describes your reaction?

❏ It's not fair, and I'm going to do something about it!

❏ I resent it, and it makes me angry, but I have to put up a good front.

❏ If that's the way it's going to be, I'll never again go the extra mile for this company!

❏ It's not fair, but maybe it'll be my turn next.

❏ I'm disappointed, but I'm going to trust God with this.

If you were to face that situation again someday, how might you handle it differently?

_____

_____

9. Jacob's own grandfather Abraham (formerly called Abram) tried to help God fulfill his promises to him. What promise did God make to Abram (Genesis 15:1-5)?

_____

_____

How did Abraham and Sarah try to fulfill God's promise themselves (Genesis 16:1-4a)?

_____

_____

What consequences were there (Genesis 16:4b-16)?

_____

Why did Abraham laugh when God restated his promise to bless Abraham (Genesis 17:15-17)?

_____

_____

How was God's promise fulfilled (Genesis 21:1-3)? Why do you suppose God waited this long to fulfill his promise to Abraham?

_____

_____

Surely Jacob knew the story of his father's birth. What lesson should he have learned from Isaac?

_____

_____

10. Have you ever seen a bit of Jacob in yourself—"helping God out"? What was the result?

_____

_____

_____

_____

Prayer

Father, when I look at Abraham, Isaac, Rebekah, and Jacob, I can so easily see their flaws and wonder why they did such foolish things. Help me to examine myself as well and see the flaws and sins I overlook or maybe even dismiss as insignificant. Shine the light of your truth on my life, and forgive me when I try to fulfill your promises on my own...

Day Two: Older but Not Wiser

Read Genesis 25:29-34.

1. Now let's examine Esau's role in this drama. What kind of condition is Esau in when Jacob proposes this bargain? Do you think his statement in verse 32 is an exaggeration or the truth? Why?

_____

_____

This week's verse to remember:

"God is no mere human! He doesn't tell lies or change his mind. God always keeps his promises." (Numbers 23:19, CEV)

2. What is he willing to give up for the sake of a meal?

_____

_____

3. Based on the description of the birthright in yesterday's question 6, what do you think might have influenced Esau to give up his birthright?

_____

_____

❧

He was defrauded
of that which he
was incapable of
appreciating.

RALPH H. ELLIOTT

4. When you look at Esau in this scene, being led astray by his appetite, what words come to mind to describe his behavior?

_____

5. We don't have to look very far to find examples of modern-day people who gave away things of lasting value—relationships, integrity, their self-esteem, their souls—to satisfy an appetite for money, pleasure, fame. Have you ever had tendencies toward Esau's temperament (on a very bad day, perhaps!)? Describe an example in your own life when you went for short-term gain instead of long-term benefit.

_____

_____

What were the consequences?

_____

_____

What lesson did you learn?

_____

_____

6. We can have a godly appetite as well. Make a note of your discoveries in each of the following verses.

Psalm 107:8-9 _____

Luke 6:21 _____

John 6:35 _____

7. Esau's actions in 25:34 are described in Hebrew with four short verbs in succession, a very unusual construction in that language. In your translation, what are those four actions?

_____

What conclusions could we draw from this stark description of Esau's behavior?

_____

_____

8. The last line of verse 34 neatly summarizes this sibling's struggle. How did Esau feel about his birthright?

_____

This is the only place in all of Genesis where this Hebrew word, translated as "despised" in the New International Version, is used. To compare, check out the following verses, and you'll see the thing that is despised has great value. In each case, what valuable "thing" is held in contempt and treated as worthless (all three of which involved King David)?

1 Samuel 17:42 _____

2 Samuel 6:16 _____

2 Samuel 12:9 _____

How would you restate that last sentence of Genesis 25:34 in your own words?

_____

9. In a sad irony, Esau himself would be despised for his actions. What does Hebrews 12:15-17 say about Esau?

_____

_____

Read Genesis 26:34-35.

10. Commentator John Hartley suggests the boys were in their late teens when the scene with the red stew took place, but by the end of the next chapter, Genesis 26:34, many years have passed. How old is Esau here, and whom has he married?

_____

Most parents are pleased when their sons marry, but what was the reaction of Isaac and Rebekah?

_____

_____

The problem is not that there were two wives but that they were Hittites; they were from a tribe of Canaanites. Earlier, in Genesis 24:1-4, Abraham had made sure that his son Isaac didn't marry a Canaanite. Why did both of these families not want their sons to marry Canaanites? Read Deuteronomy 7:1-4

_____

_____

Although God's command in Deuteronomy 7:1-4 was recorded many years after this story, what clue does it give into the problem of marrying Canaanites?

_____

_____

In what way do Esau's actions in Genesis 26:34 fit with his actions in chapter 25?

_____

_____

11. After looking at these passages regarding Esau, how would you sum up his nature? If we learn by example, what is the strongest lesson he has taught you?

_____

_____

_____

Prayer

Father, when I read the sad and stark words that Esau was rejected and could bring about no change of mind even though he sought the blessing with tears, I am so grateful that the same doesn't have to be said of me. Thank you that you do not reject me, that when I seek you in tears over my mistakes, you do not turn me away. Help me never to take for granted, or to treat casually, the blessing of being your child…

Day Three: An Aging Father, a Scheming Mother

Read Genesis 27:1-10.

1. As was the custom, Isaac prepared to give his firstborn son, Esau, his blessing. What two facts do we learn about Isaac at the start of this scene? Both play an important part in the story!

_____

_____

> *This week's verse to remember:*
> "God is no mere human! He doesn't tell lies or change his mind. God always keeps his promises." (Numbers 23:19, CEV)

2. Despite Esau's marriage to two Hittite brides, how does Isaac appear to feel about Esau? What do you base this on?

_____

_____

3. When Isaac calls him, Esau immediately responds, "Here I am." Perhaps he had an inkling of what was coming. Genesis 27:2 is an opening statement any hearer of the time would have understood to be nigh to legal terminology. What two statements does Isaac make?

_____

_____

4. In Genesis 27:3-4, what two tasks does Isaac give Esau to do?

_____

_____

And what will Isaac do for him in return?

_____

What similarities do you see between this plan and Esau and Jacob's exchange over the stew?

_____

_____

5. While Esau hunts for venison, Rebekah hunts for a solution. Why is she so determined that Jacob receive the blessing instead? What could it be compared to today?

_____

_____

_____

Blessing is the
transmission of an almost
magically
effective power of soul.
GERHARD VON RAD

Prayer

Father, I thank you that your
blessings are not limited, that you
have more love, more mercy,
more comfort than I could ever
imagine. I also thank you that I
do not have to trick you into
blessing me. I am overwhelmed
by your grace and your generosity.
Open my eyes to the blessings
that you, the giver of all good
gifts, shower upon me daily…

6. The word "blessing" appears twelve times in this chapter alone. It *really* mattered! And it still matters today. Although we may long for a blessing from our earthly parents, it is the blessing of our heavenly Father that matters most. What can we learn about those blessings from the following verses?

John 1:16 _____

Galatians 3:13-14 _____

Ephesians 1:3 _____

7. Carefully compare Isaac's words to Esau (Genesis 27:4) with Rebekah's retelling of those same words to Jacob (Genesis 27:7). What *significant* difference do you see in Rebekah's version? Why does she add those words, do you think?

_____
_____

8. Rebekah's actions beg the question, "On whose behalf is she doing this: the Lord's, her son Jacob's, or her own?" See if can you make a case for any or for all three.

For the Lord: _____

For Jacob: _____

For herself: _____

9. Much like Jacob earlier, Rebekah takes God's promise into her own hands and devises a plan to fulfill it. In what way is her plan even more cunning than Jacob's clever bartering with the lentil soup?

_____
_____
_____

10. Although Rebekah *may* have had good motives, she certainly engaged in some dubious behavior. Which of her following behaviors do you see at work in your own life?

❏ eavesdropping on a private conversation

❏ exploiting someone else's weaknesses for her own gain

❏ invoking the Lord's name to strengthen her words

❏ assuming she knows what's best for her grown child and directing his actions

❏ taking the fulfillment of God's promise into her own hands

What one step could you take to begin changing this tendency?

_____

Day Four: A Hairy Plan

Read Genesis 27:8-17.

1. Genesis 27:8 indicates that Rebekah had a plan. Does she give Jacob the option of *not* obeying her? What does that tell us about their relationship, even though he is very much a grown man at this point?

_____

_____

> *This week's verse to remember:*
> "God is no mere human! He doesn't tell lies or change his mind. God always keeps his promises." (Numbers 23:19, CEV)

2. In Genesis 27:9, Rebekah repeats once more the request that Isaac made of Esau as she stated it in Genesis 27:7, this time with a *subtle* difference. What is it?

_____

_____

Why do you think she would have dared try so risky a substitution?

_____

_____

3. Now Jacob responds to his mother's wild plan. What is Jacob worried about?

_____

What does he *not* express concern about (all those practical questions you and I might have asked!)?

_____

_____

4. His mother's initial response in Genesis 27:13 is shocking. What does she say?

_____

_____

Oh, Rebekah! Look up Genesis 4:9-12 for a sense of what it meant to be cursed by God. According to those verses, who was cursed and why?

_____

_____

And how does that cursed young man respond in Genesis 4:13?

_____

_____

Why would Rebekah have made such an outrageous statement?

_____

_____

> She operates behind the scenes, but she controls the action.
> CHRISTIANA DE GROOT

5. The following verses remind us to keep our motives and actions pure. Look up each passage and jot down what it says to you about deceiving others:

Proverbs 14:8 _____

Proverbs 24:28 _____

Romans 16:17-18 _____

2 Corinthians 4:1-2 _____

6. Although we might not plan as elaborate a deception as Rebekah's, what are some more subtle ways we intentionally deceive other people?

_____

_____

7. We are also cautioned by Scripture not to deceive ourselves. What do the following verses teach you about self-deception?

1 Corinthians 3:18-20 _____

James 1:22-25 _____

1 John 1:8_____

8. Which situation is harder for you to watch: one person deliberately deceiving another, or someone foolishly deceiving himself? Why is that?

_____

_____

Which is the easier trap for you to fall into? Why?

_____

_____

9. We tend to treat some levels of deception and lies as minor sins. Flattery, white lies, pulling the wool over someone's eyes—surely they don't rank with murder and adultery! But read John 8:44. Restate in your own words how much God hates lying.

_____

_____

By contrast, how does Paul describe the children of God in Ephesians 5:8-10?

_____

_____

10. Is there any place in your life where deception or a lie has taken root—perhaps even a self-deception? What change do you need to make?

_____

_____

_____

Prayer

Father, I want to rid my life of any desire to deceive others or myself. Help me to take the truth as seriously as you do. Please guide my thoughts, my words, my actions so that the father of lies cannot gain any foothold in me. I want to be solely your child, a child of light...

20

Day Five: Blessings for the Deceiver

Read Genesis 27:18-29.

1. Rebekah is left to wring her hands while Jacob puts their deceitful plan in motion. In the dialogue between the aging father and scheming son, what questions or concerns does Isaac raise?

   _____

   _____

This week's verse to remember:

"God is no mere human! He doesn't tell lies or change his mind. God always keeps his promises." (Numbers 23:19, CEV)

2. Now count how many lies Jacob tells, as recorded in these few verses. List as many as you can find (there are often two in a single sentence!).

   _____

   _____

   _____

3. Read Genesis 27:20 again. One biblical commentator, Meredith Kline, said of that verse, "The deceiver...spoke more truth than he realized." What might Dr. Kline mean by that?

   _____

   _____

   And what might this verse tell us about Jacob and his relationship with God at this point?

   _____

   _____

4. Skim through Genesis 27:18-26. How many times does Isaac use the words "my son" in your translation? _____ Surprised at the number? What might be the significance of Isaac's repetition of these words?

   _____

   _____

   In the passages that you have read this week, who is the only person that Rebekah calls "my son"? What interaction does she have with Esau in these passages?

   _____

   _____

5. His meat and wine consumed, Isaac puts Jacob to the test once again. In the NIV, Genesis 27:26 is the first time the word "kiss" appears in the Bible. Why do you suppose Isaac requests a kiss? How might Proverbs 24:26 help answer this question?

   _____

   _____

An abundant measure of [rain] was especially precious in a country where the rain is confined to two seasons of the year.
JAMES G. MURPHY

What New Testament example does this remind you of involving a kiss, an identity, and a betrayal?

_____

6. Genesis 27:28-29 recounts Isaac's brief but powerful blessing of Jacob. Jot down all the blessing includes.

_____

_____

How does Isaac's blessing parallel God's promise to Rebekah stated in Genesis 25:23?

_____

Which of the four statements that God made to Rebekah was already starting to be fulfilled?

_____

7. Think back over the events we've covered this week. How would you sum up this dysfunctional family? Whom did you relate to the most?

❏ the doting, gullible Isaac

❏ the dramatic, manipulative Rebekah

❏ the clever, deceitful Jacob

❏ the short-sighted, impulsive Esau

What lesson can you learn from that person?

_____

_____

8. From what you have seen of Jacob's behavior thus far, what has Jacob done to earn or deserve the blessings and favor of God?

_____

Why at this point in the story is God still in the process of honoring his promise to make Jacob's descendants a great nation?

_____

♥ 9. The biblical writers described God's faithfulness toward his people with many different word pictures. What different aspect of his faithfulness does each of the following images convey?

Psalm 121:3-4 _____

Isaiah 49:14-16 _____

Jeremiah 33:19-21 _____

Hebrews 6:16-19 _____

WEEK ONE: SIBLING RIVALRY

Which image speaks to your heart the most? Why?

_____

_____

10. Select one of God's promises you find in Scripture that you want to trust more. Then state it in your own words and personalize what that promise means to you.

Because God's Word says in _____ that he _____, then

I can trust him to_____.

If the story stopped right here, we'd have quite a mess on our hands. And there are more lies and deceit to come! But God's will *will* prevail, and his promises will not fail.

After Your Group Discussion...

The main principles or truths I learned this week are...

I want to apply these truths to my life by...

Prayer

Father, thank you that I have not come to the end of the story— not theirs and not mine. Help me to learn from their lives and from your Word. Help me to trust that you keep your promises even when I don't, that you bless me even though I am not worthy, that you love me even when I am unlovable. I praise you for being the one and only constant in life...

Video Notes

Insights:

Running from God

God Knows All About Prodigal Children

GENESIS 27:30–28:9

Running from God

God Knows All About Prodigal Children

Read Genesis 27:30–28:9.

Major events:

- Esau returns in time to learn that Jacob has received his father's blessing.

- Furious, Esau threatens to kill Jacob after their father dies.

- Rebekah tells Jacob to run for his life to her brother Laban in Haran.

- Isaac urges Jacob to seek a wife among his cousins in Haran.

- Esau makes yet another blunder, choosing another wife.

This week's verse to remember:
"The unfailing love of the LORD never ends! By his mercies we have been kept from complete destruction. Great is his faithfulness; his mercies begin afresh each day."
(Lamentations 3:22-23, NLT)

veryone has known—and some of us have *been*—a prodigal. The original meaning of "prodigal" stems from the notion of "wasteful extravagance," describing a person who carelessly handles something of great value. Because of the New Testament story of the prodigal son (Luke 15:11-32), the word has also come to mean someone who has thrown away the blessings of God with both hands, only to regret his foolishness later and return home with his hat (and little else) in his hands. Without question, Jesus' listeners would have thought of Jacob and Esau when they first heard the parable of a father and his two sons.

This week in our study, Isaac, who is now old and blind, thinks he has just passed on the blessing to his firstborn son, Esau. But both he and Esau are in for a shock. Rebekah's scheme has succeeded, and now there are consequences. Everyone in the family will pay a price, and we will see that sometimes there are no "do overs." What is spoken must be carried out. It would be a sad story indeed were it not for the promises and plans of God, which while not in the foreground of this week's events, nonetheless play the most critical role.

Since descriptions of motives and emotions are often in short supply in Scripture, we must look carefully at *what* is said and done and *how* it's said and done. Rebekah's behavior as a mature woman differs significantly from that of the young bride of Genesis 24. And while

Jacob seems to hide not only his smooth skin but his feelings as well, Isaac and Esau hold nothing back emotionally in their painful scene together after Isaac has blessed Jacob.

Clyde Francisco, in *The Broadman Bible Commentary: Genesis,* wrote, "It is almost as impossible to call back a spoken word to one's children as it is to summon a soul from the dead." As a parent, I hear that one loud and clear, and I pray my words will bless *both* my children equally and equip them to lead godly lives. One former prodigal in the family—me!—is more than enough.

Day One: A Matter of Minutes

Read Genesis 27:30-33.

1. This scene turns on a single verse: Genesis 27:30. Once again in Jacob's and Esau's lives, timing makes all the difference. Who benefits and who loses this time?

   _____

2. Note that all three men—Isaac, Jacob, Esau—are not only named in the verse, but their relationship to one another is also included—father, brothers. What purpose do you suppose all that identification serves?

   _____

   _____

3. Esau asks Isaac to sit up, just as his brother did earlier. The Hebrew word, *qum,* which appears in verse 31, literally means "to arise, to begin something." What is Esau eager for his father to do?

   _____

   _____

   Given Esau's previously cavalier attitude toward his birthright, how do you explain this keen desire he now shows for the blessing?

   _____

   _____

4. Instead, his father asks a question. How does this question differ from the one he earlier asked Jacob, back in verse 18? Do you think there is any significance in the difference? If so, explain.

   _____

   _____

5. In response, Esau identifies himself in what three ways?

_____

_____

How had Jacob responded when asked a similar question by Isaac?

_____

_____

> The tree was shaken, but it did not fall. He knew that God's will had been done.
>
> CLYDE FRANCISCO

6. The two scenes of Jacob and Esau each asking their father for his blessing have been very similar to this point. Why does Isaac respond differently to Esau's answer than he did to Jacob's?

_____

_____

7. When the truth sinks in, Isaac—a quiet, reserved man—does something rather startling...what?

_____

What emotions do you see contributing to that physical response?

_____

8. If anger is one of these possible emotions, whom might Isaac be angry with and why?

_____

_____

9. In these days of "road rage" and "air rage," we're well aware of the power of anger. What do the following passages teach us about handling anger?

Psalm 37:7-9 _____

Proverbs 29:11 _____

Ecclesiastes 7:9 _____

Ephesians 4:26-27 _____

Based on these verses—or others you've considered in the past—state in your own words how you would like to handle anger differently than you have before.

_____

_____

_____

10. Sometimes, if we're honest with ourselves, the one we're angry with is God. Perhaps Psalm 77 is one that we can relate to at such times.

According to verses 1-7, how does the psalmist feel about God at the moment?

_____

_____

According to verses 11-12, what does the psalmist choose to think about?

_____

_____

What effect would this likely have on him?

_____

_____

What traits of God does he focus on in verses 13-15?

_____

_____

The next time you are angry with God, what acts or traits of God could you focus on to gain a better perspective in the situation?

_____

_____

_____

Prayer

Heavenly Father, I confess that so often my focus is on me and what I want, and I get angry when I'm lied to or betrayed. Help me replace my anger with patience, my judgment with forgiveness, my selfishness with generosity. Teach me to extend to others the same mercy I so desperately need from you. Help me accept your will for my life and the lives of those I love…

Day Two: Bitter Tears

Read Genesis 27:34-40.

1. For the second time this day, someone has come to Isaac, claiming to be Esau, the first-born. Esau's reaction is immediate and emotional, but Warren Wiersbe suggests that "Esau's tears were not tears of repentance...they were tears of regret." What in the text would support this commentator's statement?

_____

_____

This week's verse to remember:

"The unfailing love of the LORD never ends! By his mercies we have been kept from complete destruction. Great is his faithfulness; his mercies begin afresh each day." (Lamentations 3:22-23, NLT)

2. In today's world where words are spoken lightly and contracts are often broken, it's hard to understand why this mix-up couldn't be "fixed." However, in that culture such words were binding. Perhaps James G. Murphy offers the best explanation: "The paternal benediction flowed not from the bias of the parent, but from the Spirit of God guiding his will, and therefore when so pronounced could not be revoked." In what way does each person appear to be ignoring God's role in fulfilling his promise to bless the younger son?

a. Isaac _____

b. Rebekah _____

c. Jacob _____

d. Esau _____

3. Centuries later, Esau's sad tale was still being told. How does Hebrews 12:17 describe Esau's situation?

_____

4. Whom does Isaac blame for the misplaced blessing?

_____

Various translations describe Jacob's actions as being done "treacherously" (NEB), "with subtlety" (KJV), and "with crafty cunning and treacherous deceit" (AMP). This one cuts to the chase: "Your brother tricked me" (CEV). In your opinion, to what extent was Isaac's statement accurate?

_____

_____

5. Not surprisingly, Esau also blames Jacob, whose name means "supplanter" or "deceiver." Yet what evidence of self-deception do you detect in Esau's accusation?

_____

_____

6. Three times Esau asks his father for a blessing. With Esau's tragic plight fresh in your mind, read Luke 13:23-30. What comparisons do you see between Esau's story in Genesis 27 and Jesus' teaching in Luke 13, looking at the following verses especially?

Luke 13:25 _____

Luke 13:28 _____

Luke 13:30 _____

7. Isaac does bless Esau, but his words aren't what Esau must have been hoping for. Compare Esau's blessing with Jacob's.

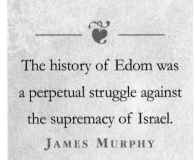

The history of Edom was a perpetual struggle against the supremacy of Israel.
JAMES MURPHY

Jacob's blessing	*Esau's blessing*
a. _____	a. _____
b. _____	b. _____
c. _____	c. _____
d. _____	d. _____
e. _____	e. _____

What positive note, if any, do you find in Esau's blessing?

_____

_____

8. To see how Esau's blessing was fulfilled—how his descendants, the Edomites, interacted with Jacob's descendants, the Israelites—note what you learn in the following verses.

Genesis 36:6 _____

Numbers 20:14-21 _____

2 Kings 8:20-22 _____

Prayer

Merciful Father, I don't want to be like Esau. I don't want to trivialize your blessings or blame others for my mistakes. I don't want to come to my senses too late about what truly is important. Please open my eyes and soften my heart toward you so that my tears are tears of repentance, not regret...

WEEK TWO

Day Three: Out for Revenge

Read Genesis 27:41-45.

1. After asking Isaac three times to bless him, Esau finally receives a dubious blessing. What is his response to his lesser blessing?

_____

Why would Esau choose to wait to act until his father dies?

_____

_____

This week's verse to remember:
"The unfailing love of the LORD never ends! By his mercies we have been kept from complete destruction. Great is his faithfulness; his mercies begin afresh each day."
(Lamentations 3:22-23, NLT)

2. We learn that some unnamed source reports Esau's plans to Rebekah. Why do you suppose Rebekah was told instead of Isaac or instead of Jacob himself? What else might that tell us about Rebekah?

_____

_____

3. Rebekah warns Jacob with this statement: "Your brother Esau is consoling himself with the thought of killing you" (NIV). By focusing on killing Jacob, what more important issues is Esau ignoring?

_____

_____

How do we sometimes take comfort in negative emotions such as anger or revenge?

_____

_____

_____

What other emotions might anger or revenge mask—emotions that are harder to deal with?

_____

4. If you have ever comforted yourself with a desire for revenge—even if you didn't seriously plan to act on it—what was the result?

_____

_____

Who paid the greatest price—you or the object of your revenge? Why?

_____

_____

At any point did you turn to God for counsel or direction? If so, what was the result?

_____

_____

If you had allowed God to handle things completely, how might that have changed the situation?

_____

_____

5. No doubt Esau was convinced he had the right to take revenge. Yet what do the following verses teach us about vengeance?

   Leviticus 19:18 _____

   Nahum 1:2-3 _____

   Romans 12:19-21 _____

6. Rebekah, meanwhile, is doing what she does best: giving orders, manipulating the situation. What three orders does she give Jacob?

   a. _____

   b. _____

   c. _____

   Haran was not a mere jog down the block but a trip of four to five hundred miles. What does this plan indicate?

   _____

   _____

7. In the first half of verse 45, Rebekah makes it clear who is to blame for Esau's anger. What do we learn about Rebekah from her comments?

   _____

   _____

8. Rebekah appears to justify her plans for Jacob with her final statement in verse 45. What possible meanings does this statement have?

   _____

   _____

9. We do not hear directly from God in the scenes we've studied this week, yet we can see him working through the events to accomplish his will. In what ways do you see his love or faithfulness or mercy in action?

   _____

   _____

   _____

10. Describe a time in which you didn't see God working in your life until long after the fact. When you did have the benefit of hindsight, how did it affect your faith?

   _____

   _____

   _____

> Her tactics are questionable, but she was not so much siding with her son against her husband as carrying out God's will for the family.
>
> CHRISTIANA DE GROOT

WEEK TWO

Prayer

Father, I can relate to Esau here; I don't want cheaters to win. Help me remember that it's not my job to see that other people get what they "deserve." Help me overcome my desire to get even or to get revenge. I sincerely want to let go of negative feelings that will only poison me...

Day Four: A Family Split

Read Genesis 27:46–28:4.

1. When Rebekah tells Jacob to flee to Laban's house, she says it is for his protection. However, her clever, cunning nature reveals itself fully in the next scene with Isaac. What did you *expect* Rebekah to tell Isaac?

_____

_____

And what does she bring up instead?

_____

_____

Why do you think she chose this tactic?

_____

_____

2. Rebekah apparently knows her husband very well. Isaac's response to her dramatic comments is precisely what she wants: Jacob safely on his way to Laban's house. Even though Jacob's safety may be her first concern, why is it important that Jacob not marry a Canaanite woman? (Look back to Day Two, question 10, of the first week, if necessary.)

_____

_____

Although Isaac and Rebekah were grieved by Esau's Hittite wives, we have no indication that they tried to stop him from marrying women from a foreign nation. What might this indicate?

_____

_____

3. Isaac, you'll remember, had no choice regarding whom he would marry; Abraham sent a servant to find God's best choice for Isaac. In the story we are studying, who was in a position to choose Jacob's wife? Put a check mark in the appropriate column for each person:

	Has a choice	Has no choice
Jacob	❏	❏
Laban	❏	❏
Laban's daughters	❏	❏

Who really is in control of this future marriage situation? How did you come to your conclusion?

_____

_____

> The Old Testament term for the church or congregation ["community of peoples," NIV] makes its first appearance.
>
> DEREK KIDNER

4. Although Isaac doesn't invoke God's name when he commands Jacob to marry one of Laban's daughters, in the very next lines Isaac calls upon God to bless Jacob. What two blessings does he ask for Jacob in this final blessing?

a. _____

b. _____

Do you see any hesitancy on Isaac's part to bless Jacob? Or any mention of his son's deception? Why might that be the case?

_____

_____

5. Remember when Rebekah boldly said, "My son, let the curse fall on me," in Genesis 27:13? A curse of sorts is indeed about to fall on her, though she will not realize it for some time: After Jacob leaves for Paddan Aram, we have no record in Scripture that Rebekah ever saw her beloved son again. But she is not the only one to suffer loss this tragic day. Note below the losses each member of the family experiences:

Isaac _____

Rebekah _____

Jacob _____

Esau _____

6. In Luke 15:11-32, Jesus tells the story of the "prodigal son." In some ways both Esau and Jacob could be described as prodigal sons.

a. In what way could it apply to Esau?

_____

_____

b. In what way could it apply to Jacob?

_____

7. Was there ever a time in your life when you were a prodigal child? If so, what were the circumstances?

_____

_____

What brought you back "home"?

_____

_____

How has that experience affected your life since?

_____

_____

Prayer

Heavenly Father, when I think about your unfailing love, I am amazed that you continue to love me even when I sin and turn my back on you or just become apathetic. I am amazed that in your mercy you continue to welcome me back. I am amazed at your faithfulness, that you never give up on me. That you would lavish all this on human beings—on me—is beyond my comprehension…

Day Five: Misguided Steps

Before we look at the last passage of Scripture for the week, let's step back and consider the bigger picture for a moment.

1. God made it clear in Genesis 25:23 that "the older will serve the younger," but do you think *this* was how God intended that truth to be lived out—with lies, deception, threats of murder, revenge, escape, and soon a hasty wedding to an unsuspecting bride? How would you explain God's willingness to work with such an untidy mess?

_____

_____

What insights does Psalm 130:1-8 provide?

_____

_____

_____

This week's verse to remember:

"The unfailing love of the LORD never ends! By his mercies we have been kept from complete destruction. Great is his faithfulness; his mercies begin afresh each day." (Lamentations 3:22-23, NLT)

♥ 2. Consider Matthew Henry's explanation: "God left [Rebekah] to herself, to take this indirect course, that he might have the glory of bringing good out of evil, and of serving his own purposes by the sins and follies of men, and that we might have the satisfaction of knowing that, though there is so much wickedness and deceit in the world, God governs it according to his will, to his own praise."

How would you restate his thoughts in your own words?

_____

_____

_____

How would you answer someone who said just the opposite—that the presence of so much wickedness in the world shows that God isn't governing it?

_____

_____

_____

What scriptures would you use to support your stance?

_____

_____

Note that Matthew Henry says God brings good out of evil so that "he might have the glory." Which are you more apt to do—praise God when good overcomes or doubt him when evil rules the day?

_____

_____

WEEK TWO: RUNNING FROM GOD

What intentional step could you take this very day to increase your praise?

_____

_____

3. The following verses describe what happens when we follow our own plans. Make a note of what each one says to you about the folly of plans made apart from God.

Isaiah 29:15-16 _____

Isaiah 30:1 _____

Jeremiah 18:11-12 _____

4. These verses address the good plans of God. What hope do you find in each one?

Psalm 33:10-11 _____

Proverbs 16:3 _____

Proverbs 19:21 _____

Jeremiah 29:11-13 _____

Read Genesis 28:5-9.

5. Jacob is sent on his way by his parents. Look carefully at all the names and places mentioned in Genesis 28:5. What is the significance of all this detailed information?

_____

_____

6. We have our last visit with Esau in these verses. Talk about irony! What does Esau learn about Jacob?

_____

_____

What does Esau realize about his father?

_____

_____

How does he address this oversight?

_____

_____

> Esau's response to this news was further evidence that he despised everything spiritual, for he went out and took another wife.
> WARREN WIERSBE

37

What do you think he was trying to achieve?

_____

_____

As we learn in Genesis 17:20-21, what was the good news–bad news about Ishmael and his descendants?

_____

_____

Prayer

All-powerful Father, I praise you for who you are—perfect love. I praise you that every good and perfect gift comes from your hand. I praise you that your glory can be seen in everything from the tiniest atom to the vastness of space. Open my eyes to see your goodness even in the smallest details and the darkest circumstances…

After Your Group Discussion…

As we close out this second week of study, what principles or insights or lessons were the most meaningful to you?

Name at least one change you would like to make as a result of your study this week (perhaps a change in attitude, or a habit you want to break, or a discipline you want to develop…).

Video Notes

Insights:

A Dream Come True

God's Love Knows No Bounds

GENESIS 28:10–22

A Dream Come True

God's Love Knows No Bounds

Read Genesis 28:10-22.

Major events:

■ On his journey Jacob dreams of a ladder of angels, stretching to heaven.

■ Jacob receives a blessing from God as well as a promise: "I am with you."

> **This week's verse to remember:**
> "God Himself has said, "I will not in any way fail you nor give you up nor leave you without support. I will not, I will not, I will not in any degree leave you helpless nor forsake nor let you down!" (Hebrews 13:5, AMP)

h, brother! We left Esau threatening to kill Jacob and Jacob preparing to run. Just as he couldn't have anticipated how that day would change his life, little does Jacob know what greater things the night will hold for him: a vivid encounter with a ladder full of angels and a Word from on high, from the God of Abraham and the God of Isaac, from a God who declares, "I am with you."

Can this be true? Almighty God, the ruler of the universe, is willing, even eager, to be with Jacob the deceiver, to watch over him wherever he goes? That's grace at work—nothing short of it. A perfect God reaching down from heaven to rescue an imperfect man. To guard and guide, protect and provide.

"But Jacob doesn't deserve you, Lord!" my petulant self whines. "He did nothing to honor your name; in fact, he woefully misused it." Careful, Liz. If God's grace were extended only to the deserving, *none* of us would qualify, for "no one is good—except God alone" (Luke 18:19). Instead, God "gives grace to the humble" (1 Peter 5:5), and "in him we have redemption through his blood, the forgiveness of sins" (Ephesians 1:7).

What a relief that is for us all! And what a revelation it must have been to Jacob to hear the voice of the Divine saying, "I will not leave you." It's an exciting turn in the biblical story—and an encouraging word of hope for those who love his name.

Day One: Divine Communication

Read Genesis 28:10-12.

1. Do you find any mention of traveling companions for Jacob? What might that suggest about his journey?

   _____

   _____

2. Despite all he has been through, Jacob falls asleep and dreams…and what a dream he has! This is not the only instance in Scripture where God spoke to someone through a dream. According to Job 33:14-18, what sort of messages does God at times convey?

   _____

   _____

3. There are other Old Testament "dreamers" we might consider. Look up the following passages and note *who* is dreaming, what God's *purpose* is, and what the *results* were:

	The dreamer	God's purpose	The result of the dream
Genesis 20:3-7	_____	_____	_____
Genesis 37:5-8	_____	_____	_____
1 Kings 3:5-15	_____	_____	_____

4. Back to Jacob. Take a moment to sketch out (yes, *draw!*) his dream as described in Genesis 28:12. Not to worry if you have zero artistic ability. I simply want you to get a clear picture of his vision in your mind by committing it to paper. (Hint: It probably wasn't a ladder with rungs but more like the sloping side of a ziggurat. Think Mayan pyramid.)

5. Jesus describes a similar "stream of messengers" in John 1:51. What might be the significance of the angels ascending and descending?

   _____

   _____

6. A band of angels coming down from heaven is not a common occurrence in either the Old or New Testament. What is their purpose in each of the following examples?

   a. Luke 2:8-14 _____

   b. Matthew 4:1-11 _____

   c. Matthew 24:29-31 _____

Loved by God

What does this suggest about Jacob, since God sent him a vision of angels as well?

_____

_____

7. Throughout Scripture, God "came down" to appear before his people. David gives a vivid description of God coming down from heaven in Psalm 18:6-15. Note below how David describes his experience, and then compare it to Jacob's vision.

	David	Jacob
What was happening in David's/Jacob's life at the time?	_____	_____
God appeared at whose initiative?	_____	_____
What was God's purpose?	_____	_____
In what form did the heavenly being appear?	_____	_____
What was David's/Jacob's relationship with God like at the time?	_____	_____

What does this tell you about God?

_____

_____

8. Read Isaiah 64:3-9, where the prophet Isaiah gives an impassioned plea for God to come down to his people.

a. What does he say God's appearing would be like?

_____

b. What would happen to sinners?

_____

c. To what does he compare man's righteous acts?

_____

d. To what was he literally referring?

_____

e. What hope do these verses offer?

_____

9. When you look at God's interaction with Jacob and David and others, what stands out most to you about the nature of God as he interacts with mankind?

_____

_____

_____

There could not have been a time when he needed more divine encouragement than now, nor a moment when he expected it less.

CLYDE FRANCISCO

Prayer

Heavenly Father, when I realize that the best thing I will ever do in my life is no better than a dirty rag to you, I know that on my own I am totally unworthy of being saved. Thank you for coming down to earth in human form so I could be saved from my sins. And thank you for sending your Holy Spirit to remain with me and to guide me…

Day Two: God's Promise and Presence

Read Genesis 28:13-16.

1. God speaks directly to Jacob in his dream and begins by identifying himself. Specifically, how does God do so?

   _____

   _____

This week's verse to remember:

"God Himself has said, 'I will not in any way fail you nor give you up nor leave you without support. I will not, I will not, I will not in any degree leave you helpless nor forsake nor let you down!'" (Hebrews 13:5, AMP)

2. Speaking of Abraham and Isaac, God had spoken to them, too. List under each man the statements and promises God made to him.

   Abraham (Genesis 15:7)

   _____

   _____

   _____

   _____

   Isaac (Genesis 26:23-24)

   _____

   _____

   _____

   _____

   Jacob (Genesis 28:13-15)

   _____

   _____

   _____

   _____

   Which statements and promises do they have in common?

   _____

   _____

   Which promises are given just to Jacob?

   _____

   _____

   Can you sense the excitement building as God continues to work out his plan to fulfill the promise he made first to Abraham!

3. That very phrase—"I am the LORD"—appears in the NIV 158 times, all in the Old Testament. It is apparent that God reached down to his people again and again, trying to get their attention, extending his unmerited grace. It is also apparent that both he and his name were to be taken seriously. What do the following verses reveal?

Exodus 20:1-7 _____

Isaiah 42:8 _____

Isaiah 43:11-13 _____

Isaiah 45:5-7 _____

This is how Exodus 20:7 reads in the Amplified Version: "You shall not use or repeat the name of the Lord your God in vain [that is, lightly or frivolously, in false affirmations or profanely]; for the Lord will not hold him guiltless who takes His name in vain."

Do you need to exercise greater care in using the Lord's name? In what ways?

_____

_____

_____

4. How do God's promises to Jacob in Genesis 28:13-14 compare to Isaac's last words to Jacob in Genesis 28:3-4?

_____

_____

_____

5. Perhaps the greatest promise God makes to Jacob is found in Genesis 28:15a. Write out the first part of that verse below. Just as God spoke those words to Jacob four thousand years ago, God speaks those same words to those who love him today:

_____

_____

How does that word from God comfort or encourage you in your present circumstances?

_____

_____

_____

In what unique way is this promise given to Christians, according to John 14:15-17?

_____

_____

> This is the greatest promise God can make to anyone.
>
> JOHN HARTLEY

6. Note one way in which each of the following passages assures you that God is with you at all times:

Psalm 23:4 _____

Psalm 42:8 _____

Psalm 118:6-7 _____

Psalm 139:7-12 _____

7. In what ways does it encourage to you to know that God is *always* with you?

_____

_____

When are you most eager to have him with you?

_____

_____

When, if ever, are you uncomfortable thinking, "God is here with me"?

_____

_____

8. The first thing that popped into Jacob's mind when he awoke from his dream was not breakfast or the long journey ahead; he thought of God. What was his statement?

_____

_____

Perhaps you're reminded of the praise chorus "Surely the presence of the LORD is in this place." The phrase "presence of the LORD" appears 34 times in the NIV translation of the Old Testament. His presence was something to be sought, yet reverently feared. Recall an incident when you were especially aware of the presence of the Lord. What brought about that awareness?

_____

_____

_____

How might you enter into his presence on a daily, even hourly, basis?

_____

_____

_____

Prayer

Holy Father, how lightly I take your presence at times. Help me to take comfort in you as my "Abba, Father," who loves and protects and guides me, but also to revere you as the only God, a holy God, and the Creator of the universe. Please guard my words and my thoughts so that I never treat your name or your presence with anything less than awe-filled respect...

WEEK THREE

Day Three: Sacred Sites

Read Genesis 28:16-17.

1. As we studied yesterday, when Jacob wakes up, he realizes that this was no ordinary dream and that he has been in the presence of God. According to verse 17, what was his immediate reaction?

   _____

   _____

This week's verse to remember:
"God Himself has said, 'I will not in any way fail you nor give you up nor leave you without support. I will not, I will not, I will not in any degree leave you helpless nor forsake nor let you down!'" (Hebrews 13:5, AMP)

   The *Holman Bible Dictionary* explains: "When God appears to a person, the person experiences the reality of God's holiness. This self-disclosure of God points to the vast distinction between humans and God, to the mysterious characteristic of God that at the same time attracts and repels." Why would God's holiness both attract and repel us?

   _____

   _____

2. The "fear of the Lord" has little to do with anxiety but a great deal to do with reverence and respect and honor. Below, you will find just a few of the verses in the NIV translation that include "the fear of the LORD." Note what each one teaches you:

   Psalm 19:9 _____

   Proverbs 1:7 _____

   Proverbs 14:27 _____

   Proverbs 16:6 _____

   Proverbs 23:17 _____

3. The phrase "the fear of the Lord" appears just once in the NIV New Testament, referring to the first-century church. How is that body of believers described in Acts 9:31, and why might fearing God have contributed to their "time of peace"?

   _____

   _____

4. The presence of the Lord and the fear of the Lord frequently go hand in hand. Ironically, God or his messenger often says, "Fear not." This is not to dissuade people from respecting and honoring God but rather an invitation to trust him. Note in the following passages to whom these words were spoken and what God was asking each to do.

   Deuteronomy 31:7-8 _____

   Jeremiah 1:1-8 _____

5. Jacob's next words—"How awesome is this place!" (NIV)—sound more contemporary than patriarchal to me! Unfortunately, "awesome" has been overused until it almost has

no power to convey its true significance anymore. But we can be sure Jacob didn't use this word lightly. He recognized that God's presence had changed the very ground on which he stood. Sound familiar? What happened in the following instances?

Exodus 3:1-5 _____

Leviticus 16:1-2 _____

6. As stated in 2 Corinthians 6:16-18, God now dwells among us. We, too, should be changed by his presence. Personalize this passage by writing it out below and inserting your name as if God were saying it directly to you. I'll get you started.

_____ is the temple of the living God. As I have said, "I will live with _____ and walk with her, and… _____

_____

Because we have this promise of God dwelling with us, how does Paul say it should change our lives (2 Corinthians 7:1)?

_____

_____

7. With a final look at Genesis 28:17, we see that Jacob declares he has seen the "gate of heaven." This is the only place that exact phrase appears in the NIV, but you'll find other important "gates" described in the New Testament. Note what the two passages below reveal about Jesus Christ, our own "gate of heaven."

John 10:9_____

Matthew 7:13-14 _____

8. If "only a few" find that gate, how can you be certain you have walked through the "right gate," the one that leads to eternal life?

_____

_____

What insights do the following verses give?

Romans 10:9-10 _____

1 John 5:12-13 _____

9. In your own words explain how we should "fear the Lord." Can you think of a parallel situation or a metaphor that might help an unbeliever understand the difference between a "healthy" and "unhealthy" fear of the Lord?

_____

_____

_____

How will a right fear of the Lord affect our relationship with him?

_____

_____

In pagan belief a site was sacred from primordial time, but in Scripture a site never became endowed with sacredness; a particular place was holy only as long as God chose to reveal himself there.
JOHN HARTLEY

Prayer

Awesome Father, to be honest, it frightens me to think that you dwell with me. My words, my thoughts, my actions aren't holy, aren't pure. Help me have a more constant awareness of your presence *in* me and *with* me so that your goodness may show *through* me…

Day Four: More Than a Name Change

Read Genesis 28:18-21.

1. After this incredible night in which God has spoken to him, Jacob turns his pillow into a pillar. What was the significance?

_____

_____

Why does he pour oil on it? What insight does Exodus 30:23-29 provide?

_____

_____

2. He also changes the name of that sacred place to Bethel, or *Beth-El,* which in Hebrew means "House of God." We don't put as much significance in names today, but in Jacob's time names were chosen not to sound good but to reveal the nature of who or what was being named. (Remember Hairy and Heel?) And *changing* a name signified a transformation in character or destiny. Although Jacob is changing the name of the *place,* what transformation is occurring in *him?* What indicates this?

_____

_____

I like the British tradition of naming one's home—Rose Cottage, Bridgeview, Abbeyside. Consider giving your home a name to express the essence of what you would like your family, friends, neighbors—your Creator—to find there. What name would you give it?

_____

What changes would you make in your home to bring about the transformation?

_____

_____

The biblical concept of naming was rooted in the ancient world's understanding that a name expressed essence. To know the name of a person was to know that person's total character and nature.

HOLMAN BIBLE DICTIONARY

3. *Bethel* appears dozens of times in Scripture after Jacob renamed it, in some cases parenthetically—Genesis 35:6 says "Luz (that is, Bethel)" and Joshua 16:2 reads "Bethel (that is, Luz)." Check out the following two verses from Genesis 35. Although this scene falls beyond the time boundary of our study, note how God describes what happened at Bethel and then how Jacob views that event.

God in Genesis 35:1 _____

Jacob in Genesis 35:2-3 _____

How does Genesis 28:20-21 verify that Jacob is a changed man by this time?

_____

_____

_____

_____

4. Not only did Bethel represent "God's house" to Jacob, it was also where he made a vow to God. What five expectations does Jacob place on God?

a. _____

b. _____

c. _____

d. _____

e. _____

Does this sound presumptuous to you? I am taken aback by Jacob's words, and then I realize how I tend to do the same thing. God offers me heaven and eternal life with him, and I say, "That's great, but I'd be more interested in following you if you made things easier for me here on earth—a little more money, a little less trouble, and no suffering, please. And, by all means, don't ask me to be a missionary!" Oh, I may not say it that candidly, but my actions do. What about you? What stipulations are you putting on God before you are willing to wholeheartedly follow him?

_____

_____

_____

5. How has God already promised each of these things directly or indirectly to Jacob?

_____

_____

What do these statements from Jacob indicate about him?

_____

_____

_____

6. What does Jacob promise to do in return?

_____

_____

7. Jacob vows to do even more than that, as we'll see in a moment, but this is the most momentous promise Jacob makes to God. In truth, it is the most life-changing commitment any of us can make before God. Write out Jacob's brief statement below in your own words. Then read it aloud as though God were present in the room with you…because he is!

_____

_____

_____

8. What does it mean to you, to claim God as *your* God? How could you demonstrate that commitment to him on a daily basis?

_____

_____

_____

Prayer

Gracious Father, your generosity toward me is pure grace. I deserve nothing, yet my prayers are more often filled with requests than praise and thanksgiving. So I stop right now and praise you for your grace and thank you for having already given me everything that is important—salvation through your Son, Jesus Christ…

Day Five: Jacob's Promises and Offerings

Read Genesis 28:22.

1. Jacob goes on to make two more promises to God. What are they?

_____

_____

2. This is not the first time the giving of a tenth, or tithe, is mentioned in the Bible. For that story, read Genesis 14:18-23. To whom did Abram (before God changed his name to Abraham) spontaneously present a tithe, and why?

_____

_____

3. Moses will later record the tithe as law in Leviticus. According to the following verses, what is to be tithed to God?

Leviticus 27:30 _____

Leviticus 27:32 _____

4. The people of God grew careless about their giving (sound familiar?), so God spoke to them through the prophet Malachi. Read Malachi 3:6-12, and then answer the following questions.

What does God accuse his people of doing?

_____

_____

What does God tell them to do instead?

_____

_____

And what promises does God make if they do so?

_____

_____

5. Fast-forward to the New Testament. Let's see if God tells us how much we are to give as believers of Jesus Christ. What do the following verses suggest we are to give to God?

1 Corinthians 16:1-2 _____

2 Corinthians 9:7 _____

6. How might you explain the fact that the words *tenth* and *tithe* do not appear in these verses?

_____

_____

What insight does Matthew 23:23 give to the answer?

_____

_____

7. If your present level of giving to God doesn't correspond with the New Testament directives Paul wrote to the Corinthians, what specific steps do you need to take to become a more *generous* giver?

_____

_____

And what steps do you need to take to become a more *cheerful* giver?

_____

_____

♥ What scriptures other than those already mentioned could serve as a good reminder to you as you plan your giving?

_____

_____

_____

> By making such a contribution a person concretely expressed God's lordship over all one's property.
>
> **JOHN HARTLEY**

After Your Group Discussion…

After nearly three full weeks of study, we finally see a major turnaround starting in Jacob! As you have studied Jacob's character to this point, and God's interaction with him, what principle stands out most in your mind?

Having studied these verses this week, what changes do you want to apply in your life?

Prayer

Father, help me willingly, even joyfully release my "things" to you. Even though I realize they become a burden sometimes, I don't give them up easily. Help me experience the joy of accepting that everything belongs to you—including my money, my time, my life…

Video Notes

Insights:

Blinded by Love

Man Looks at the Outward Appearance; God Looks at the Heart

GENESIS 29:1–20

Blinded by Love

Man Looks at the Outward Appearance; God Looks at the Heart

Read Genesis 29:1-20.

Major events:

■ Jacob questions the local shepherds at a well and asks about his Uncle Laban.

■ Jacob meets his cousin Rachel, waters her sheep, and follows her home.

■ Jacob strikes a bargain for the hand of his beloved Rachel.

> **This week's verse to remember:**
> "Guide my steps by your word, so I will not be overcome by any evil. Rescue me from the oppression of evil people; then I can obey your commandments. Look down on me with love; teach me all your principles." (Psalm 119:133-135, NLT)

Jacob's journey east continues, and what a l-o-n-g trek it is, although not a day of it is described in Scripture. The climax of the trip takes place at a well with three flocks of sheep on hand, some taciturn shepherds, and a certain shepherdess by the name of Rachel. Before the scene ends with tears and a kiss, Jacob will surprise his onlookers with a feat of strength worthy of Samson wooing Delilah.

Rachel runs to tell her father the good news that a relative has arrived, and Laban hurries to meet his nephew. Is it just me, or is this a more energetic branch of the family? Poor Isaac has to be told, "Sit up! Sit up!" while effusive Laban is on his feet and making tracks.

This week we'll consider Laban's warm welcome and what expectations he might have concerning his visiting nephew, and we'll look at Jacob's quick assimilation into the home of his relatives. The word for Jacob is *willing:* willing to work, willing to marry, willing to wait, willing to work some more. His Aramean uncle, grateful for the free labor, is in no hurry to see Jacob pick up his heels and move back home with one of Laban's daughters in tow.

Oh, did we mention the daughters? This week we'll get to know them, at least by name: Leah, the older one with unusual eyes (are they "weak" or "tender" or "sparkling"?), and Rachel, the younger sister, who is "beautiful of form and face" (NASB). Guess which one Jacob decides he loves? And guess what outrageous bride-price the smitten man is willing to pay?

Laban is elated, although he hides it well. "Stay," Laban says, and Jacob does. Time flies. Months are mere minutes. In a single verse, seven years pass. Jacob has fulfilled his duty as a laborer; now he would fulfill his role as a husband.

Day One: Journey's End

Read Genesis 29:1-9.

1. Leaving Bethel behind, Jacob presses east toward Paddan Aram. Verse 1 literally covers nearly five hundred miles! Why do you think that long, arduous journey was not described in detail for us in Scripture? (There are no right or wrong answers here; just give it some thought.)

   _____

   _____

2. Based on God's promises and Jacob's vows at Bethel that we studied last week, what do we know *for certain* about Jacob's journey?

   _____

   _____

3. As Jacob approaches Haran, he comes to a well in the field. Who and what are waiting at the well?

   _____

   What do we learn about the well itself?

   _____

   What possible reason(s) might you offer for Jacob's stopping here first rather than pressing on to his uncle's home?

   _____

   _____

4. To help you step inside Jacob's sandals for a moment, recall a specific time in your adulthood when you were the "new face in town"—in a new neighborhood, a new job, a new church. Any awkward, first-time situation will do. What strategy did *you* use to introduce and ingratiate yourself to that group of strangers?

   _____

   _____

5. In Jacob's brief conversation with the shepherds, he asks simple questions, and they give him *very* brief answers. In your translation, what does Jacob *call* the men? _____. Why might he have done so?

_____

_____

Do they initially offer him any information beyond what he asks of them? _____ What might that indicate?

_____

_____

6. Then the shepherds provide some useful information without being asked. What do they tell Jacob?

_____

_____

Is it good news or bad news…and why?

_____

_____

7. Jacob responds to their announcement with a surprising suggestion, particularly for a visiting stranger. What does he tell them to do?

_____

_____

Various biblical commentators are quite certain why Jacob asked them to do this. Given only the information we have in the text, what do *you* think Jacob was up to?

_____

_____

Is Jacob back to his old, deceptive ways? Why or why not?

_____

_____

8. The shepherds tell him two things must happen before their sheep will be watered:

_____

_____

But as they're talking, Jacob's attention is no longer focused on the shepherds, the sheep, or the well. Who shows up?

_____

He tries to rid the scene of onlookers even before he has a clue to Rachel's incandescent beauty.
ROSE SALBERG KAM

What do we learn about this newcomer in that single verse?

_____

_____

9. Even in this short episode, we see God at work guiding Jacob and being "with him."
   Note below at least four indications you see of God's handiwork in these events.

   a. _____

   b. _____

   c. _____

   d. _____

10. How is God turning Jacob's desperate situation—running for his life—into a blessing?

_____

_____

_____

Prayer

Merciful Father, how I love to know you are guiding my steps! What peace and comfort that brings. I praise you for those times when I can see your guiding hand. Help me trust you more in those times when I'm uncertain. As the psalmist said, I ask you to guide me through your Word so that I won't be overcome by evil...

WEEK FOUR

Loved by God

Read Genesis 29:10-11.

1. We have no record of what Jacob said to the new arrival…only what he did. How would you explain this remarkable feat?

_____

_____

This week's verse to remember:

"Guide my steps by your word, so I will not be overcome by any evil. Rescue me from the oppression of evil people; then I can obey your commandments. Look down on me with love; teach me all your principles." (Psalm 119:133-135, NLT)

---

2. We have more surprises in store! Verse 11 describes a rather emotional display on Jacob's part. In the Old Testament close relatives would kiss upon greeting or departing from each other as a sign of acceptance, but what else might have prompted this kiss?

_____

_____

Why do you think Jacob wept?

_____

_____

3. There is no shame in a man weeping. According to Scripture, many of God's bravest, strongest men wept. Who is crying in the following verses, and why?

	Who wept…	…and why?
Genesis 43:30	_____	_____
		_____
1 Samuel 30:3-4	_____	_____
		_____
Jeremiah 9:1	_____	_____
		_____
Matthew 26:75	_____	_____
		_____
John 11:32-36	_____	_____
		_____

4. Repentance often produces tears. What does 2 Chronicles 34:27 tell us about how God responds to our humble tears?

_____

_____

In rolling the stone from the well by himself, Jacob was risking the wrath of the whole community.

CLYDE FRANCISCO

5. Perhaps Jacob was simply overcome with God's faithfulness in bringing him safely to Paddan Aram. What do the following verses teach us about the faithfulness of God?

Deuteronomy 7:9 _____

_____

Psalm 86:15 _____

_____

Psalm 119:89-90 _____

_____

Isaiah 25:1 _____

6. Have you ever been overwhelmed by the *faithfulness* of God, even to the point of weeping? Describe such a time in your life and how that memory encourages you to remain faithful to God.

_____

_____

_____

_____

Prayer

Father, I thank you for tears of joy—when my heart is so full that I can't hold them back—and I ask you to keep my heart tender. I want to rejoice with those who rejoice and weep with those who weep. I especially want my heart to be tender to your nudging so that I am quick to repent when I sin...

Day Three: Jacob Meets His Match

Read Genesis 29:12-15.

1. Freshly kissed, Rachel starts running, and her father, Laban, starts hurrying. What reasons could you offer for Rachel's eagerness to share the news of her cousin's arrival?

_____

_____

_____

And what of her father, Laban? List some reasons why he might be in a hurry to see his nephew.

_____

_____

Read Genesis 24:28-31, which describes Abraham's messenger selecting Rebekah for Isaac. What clue to Laban's character and motivation does this meeting provide?

_____

_____

2. Laban welcomed Jacob with open arms. In what ways did Laban demonstrate his enthusiasm?

_____

_____

3. What might "all these things" (NIV) that Jacob told his Uncle Laban include? It is clear that he volunteered the information. How much of his story do you think Jacob told Laban, and what makes you say that?

_____

_____

_____

Paraphrase the following verses in one sentence each. How could heeding these admonitions have served Jacob well that day?

Proverbs 17:28 _____

_____

_____

_____

_____

This week's verse to remember:

"Guide my steps by your word, so I will not be overcome by any evil. Rescue me from the oppression of evil people; then I can obey your commandments. Look down on me with love; teach me all your principles." (Psalm 119:133-135, NLT)

Tradition has it that when Laban ran out to greet Jacob, embracing and kissing him, it was solely to discover the money and gems he felt certain that this beloved member of Abraham's household would come bearing as gifts.

BARBARA L. RONSON

Proverbs 21:23 _____

_____

_____

_____

_____

Proverbs 29:20 _____

_____

_____

_____

_____

4. Most of us could profit from these verses as well. Which of the following is the greatest temptation for you?

- ❏ giving advice too freely

- ❏ dominating conversations

- ❏ interrupting others rather than patiently listening

- ❏ flattering others

- ❏ cutting others off if you disagree

- ❏ speaking rashly in anger

- ❏ being quick to divulge others' sins

- ❏ revealing too much to people before you know they can be trusted

- ❏ stretching the truth

Memorize one of the three proverbs mentioned in question 3—or a verse like James 1:19—and commit to work this week on improving in this area. Consider asking a trusted friend or family member to help by holding you accountable to your resolution to guard your tongue and speak with discretion.

5. It's clear that Jacob stays with Laban and works for a full month. Since Jacob's skills include shepherding and Laban clearly owns sheep, we can assume caring for them might have been Jacob's job. How much does Laban pay Jacob for his labors?

_____

Read Deuteronomy 24:14-15 to discover how God said workers were to be paid. *Note:* Although the events recorded in Deuteronomy came several hundred years after those in Genesis, it's important to remember that (1) the Pentateuch (the first five books of the Bible) were all written around 1400 B.C. and (2) Deuteronomy includes laws of the people that were commonly accepted and had been in place for centuries.

What did God direct employers to do? Why?

_____

_____

Given the directive in these verses, how do you view the situation at hand? Is Jacob being generous with his time—a month of free labor—or is Laban being stingy with his funds? Offer a plausible explanation for Jacob's working thirty days without pay.

_____

_____

_____

6. Jot down Laban's request as stated in verse 15:

_____

_____

This is the first place in the NIV where we find the word "wages." It will appear seven times in Genesis, each time involving these same two men. How might a similar discussion between Jacob and Laban many years later, as recorded in Genesis 30:27-30, reveal how each man honored his commitment concerning work and wages? Also read Genesis 29:16-30 for your answer.

_____

_____

7. Jacob, himself a deceiver, perhaps does not realize at this point what Laban's true motives are and what his plans are for Jacob. What evidence do we see of Jacob's relying on God as he lives with and works for Laban?

_____

_____

After the powerful experience Jacob had at Bethel, how do you explain his current self-reliance?

_____

_____

Day Four: Beauty Seen and Unseen

Read Genesis 29:16-17.

1. On the heels of the word "wages" comes the introduction of Laban's two daughters. No coincidence, this. Without reading ahead or peeking at any study notes your Bible might contain, write down everything you know (or think you know!) about these two famous sisters. No right or wrong here; this is a matter of perceptions and preconceived notions.

This week's verse to remember:

"Guide my steps by your word, so I will not be overcome by any evil. Rescue me from the oppression of evil people; then I can obey your commandments. Look down on me with love; teach me all your principles." (Psalm 119:133-135, NLT)

Leah   Rachel

_____   _____

_____   _____

_____   _____

2. "Older" and "younger"—now *that* should ring a bell. Esau and Jacob were born only seconds apart. Are we told how many months or years separate the two sisters?

_____

If you have siblings, what observations could you share about those who are close in age—say, one to three years—and those who are farther apart?

_____

_____

_____

3. The girls are described with only a handful of words. First, let's look at Leah. What does the Word of God say about Leah, the older sister?

_____

_____

Clearly this information matters to the story, or it would not have been included. But *why* did it matter? What might that tell us about Leah—physically, emotionally, spiritually? How might the condition of her eyes affect her appearance, her domestic skills, her ability to be a wife and mother? Jot down everything that specific attribute might indicate about Leah.

_____

_____

_____

4. When we met Esau and Jacob at their births, Esau was indeed described physically. When we met the twins again as young men, in Genesis 25:27, what was the emphasis?

_____

_____

Do you see a similar dichotomy still in place four thousand years later? How do we frequently define women? How do we often define men? Why do you believe this is done?

_____

_____

5. According to the following verses, how does God view people? Restate each passage briefly in your own words and personalize it. (The first one is done as an example.) Try reading the passages in more than one version to see which wording is most meaningful to you.

   a. 1 Samuel 16:7—People will judge me by how I look, but the Lord sees my thoughts and my intentions.

   b. Proverbs 31:30 _____

_____

   c. Isaiah 66:2 _____

_____

   d. 1 Peter 3:3-4 _____

_____

If you are in a small group, have members share various translations and their own "paraphrases."

♥ 6. We don't know much about Jesus' physical appearance when he was on earth, but Isaiah 53:2-3 gives us a clue. How does the passage describe Jesus' appearance?

_____

_____

Considering that Jesus could have come in any likeness God desired, why do you think he chose this one?

_____

> Perhaps Rachel is more outwardly beautiful, but Leah is more sensitive and kind.
>
> ALICE OGDEN BELLIS

7. Now let's take a closer look at Rachel. When she first arrives on the scene with her sheep, Rachel's comely looks are not described, though Jacob certainly does respond positively to seeing her. But the later verses leave no question about her appearance. How does your translation describe Rachel?

_____

_____

With the use of the word "but," it appears that Leah and Rachel are being contrasted. What differences does the text state or imply?

_____

_____

8. A woman's beauty is an integral element in several Old Testament stories. Take a brief look at the following passages and make note of what you find there.

	Who is beautiful?	Why might that be dangerous?
Genesis 12:10-13	_____	_____
Genesis 26:6-7	_____	_____
2 Samuel 11:2-4	_____	_____

9. In your experiences, have you seen a situation where a woman's beauty led to trouble?

_____

Given what we've seen in Scripture and know to be true in our own lives, how might Rachel's beauty point to future problems for Jacob?

_____

_____

10. Physical beauty doesn't have to lead to trouble. We see in Esther 2:15-17 that Esther used her beauty—combined with courage—for godly purposes. How else might a woman's beauty be used of God for his glory?

_____

_____

_____

11. Take a personal inventory by comparing your outward beauty care with your inward beauty care. List below what you do daily or weekly to enhance your beauty in each area.

Physical beauty regimen   Spiritual beauty regimen

_____   _____

_____   _____

_____   _____

_____   _____

Are your regimens in the proper balance? If not, what adjustments could you make?

_____

_____

_____

Prayer

Heavenly Father, I want to become a beautiful woman in your sight. Help me look at myself and see what you see—my heart, my thoughts, my attitudes. And in those areas where I need a beauty makeover, guide me in your regimen for transforming my spirit. Thank you for being patient with me and for not giving up on me, even when I am the most unlovely...

WEEK FOUR

Day Five: The Price of Love

Read Genesis 29:18-20.

1. Whether it was love at first sight—that kiss by the well—or whether it took a month for him to know his feelings, Jacob's affection for Rachel is clearly stated. In our first week together we learned that Isaac loved Rebekah (Genesis 24:67). There are only a few scattered mentions in the Old Testament of such romantic feelings between men and women—Elkanah loved Hannah (1 Samuel 1:4-5), and Michal loved David (1 Samuel 18:20). But nearly all of the 733 appearances in the NIV of the words "love," "loves," "loving," or "loved" refer to God's loving us or to our being called to love one another. A great example of both can be found in 1 John 4:7-12. State at least three principles about love that you find in these verses.

   a. _____

   b. _____

   c. _____

2. We say that we "love God," and you probably say "I love you" to certain people—a spouse, a parent, a child. Surely these emotions, and the practical ways they are expressed, are not identical. How would you describe your love for God and your love for a certain person who is dear to you? Circle any words that appear in both columns.

   Love for God   Love for _____

   _____   _____

   _____   _____

   _____   _____

   _____   _____

   How might your love for God enhance the earthly relationship you've listed here?

   _____

   _____

   Does your love for God strain that relationship in any way?

   _____

   The following verses teach us how to love others in a way that's pleasing to God. Note a brief, helpful lesson from each one.

   John 13:34-35 _____

   1 Peter 1:22-23_____

   1 John 3:18 _____

   1 John 4:20-21 _____

3. Now look back over Genesis 29:1-18, beginning right after Jacob's personal encounter with God.

   Is there any mention of God in these eighteen verses? _____

   Does Jacob thank God, as Abraham's servant did, for guiding him? _____

   Does Jacob offer praises to him for beautiful Rachel? _____

   After reviewing those verses, what conclusion(s) might you draw about Jacob and his relationship with God at this point in the story?

   _____

   _____

4. Laban, you'll remember, asked Jacob what his wages should be. Now Jacob states how long he is willing to work, that is, _____, and his expected compensation, namely, _____. What detail does Jacob include, lest there be any question which daughter he means?

   _____

5. Laban's response is curious. How would you interpret Laban's answer to Jacob's offer?

   _____

   _____

   And what does Laban *not* say that you might have expected?

   _____

   _____

6. Jacob is a man of his word here; we learn that he fulfills his part of the bargain. Perhaps you've held the same job for seven years; imagine working all those years *without getting paid!* Clyde Francisco wrote, "No man who loved that unselfishly could be an essentially self-centered person." Do you agree…or disagree? Have we seen Jacob behave unselfishly before? If not, how might you explain his behavior here?

   _____

   _____

   _____

7. Especially when compared to today's marital standards, Jacob's commitment to wait and work for Rachel is remarkable. While we may not be asked to sacrifice seven years of hard labor for someone we love, we are asked to make daily sacrifices in the name of love. According to the following verses, in what specific and practical ways are we to show love to those around us?

   Leviticus 19:18 _____

   Proverbs 10:12 _____

   Proverbs 17:9 _____

Custom regards the father of the bride as entitled to some compensation for the trouble had in her training, and for the loss of service experienced by her departure from home. If this compensation cannot be rendered in money, jewels, or cattle, it may be given in labor.

JAMES M. FREEMAN

WEEK FOUR

Matthew 5:44 _____

Romans 12:9-18 _____

1 Peter 3:8_____

Select one of these practical ways to show love and commit to expressing it to someone today.

After Your Group Discussion...

Restate in your own words the most important principles you learned this week.

How will you respond to these truths?

Video Notes

Insights:

A Deceiver Deceived

God Disciplines the Ones He Loves

GENESIS 29:21–29

A Deceiver Deceived

God Disciplines the Ones He Loves

Read Genesis 29:21-29.

Major events:

■ After seven years of labor, Jacob is more than ready to be married.

■ On the wedding night Laban secretly presents Leah—not Rachel—to eager Jacob.

■ The next morning Jacob discovers his father-in-law's deceit and protests loudly.

■ Laban blames local custom and strikes a second deal for Rachel's hand.

This week's verse to remember:
"My child, don't ignore it when the LORD disciplines you, and don't be discouraged when he corrects you. For the LORD corrects those he loves, just as a father corrects a child in whom he delights." (Proverbs 3:12, NLT)

hen Isaac and Rebekah sent their younger son, Jacob, off to Paddan Aram to marry one of Laban's daughters, they surely did not foresee a turnabout like *this* one…nor did Jacob! If this story is new to you, Laban's deceptive move no doubt caught you by surprise as well. Even those of us who knew what was coming still shake our heads with more questions than answers as we read this cruel twist in the story.

Our lesson this week will inch along through only nine verses. As we grapple with the myriad issues at hand—ethical, moral, legal, sexual, emotional, and spiritual —we must remind ourselves that we're studying the story of *one* family in a specific time and place, a family greatly influenced by their primitive culture and their developing faith in the one true God within a polytheistic society (one that worshiped many pagan gods).

Having said all that, we *can* learn from this unseemly situation and can apply these lessons to our lives. Paul assures us that "all Scripture is God-breathed and is useful for teaching, rebuking, correcting and training in righteousness, so that the man of God may be thoroughly equipped for every good work" (2 Timothy 3:16-17). Much as we might be tempted to put aside some stories in the Bible and say, "No thanks. That one doesn't appeal or apply to me," the truth is, every story in some way points to our fallible human nature and our desperate need for a Savior.

The key is not to get so caught up in studying the lives of people in the Bible that we forget to examine our own lives, our own failings, our own motives, our own need for repentance. Jesus cautioned the Jews who were persecuting him, "You diligently study the Scriptures because you think that by them you possess eternal life. These are the Scriptures that testify about me, yet you refuse to come to me to have life" (John 5:39-40). As you study this week, come to the Scriptures to learn, and come to the Savior to discover what unique lessons he has for *you* that will draw you closer to him.

Day One: A Big Switch

Read Genesis 29:21-23.

1. After the seven long years come to an end, Jacob tells Laban to uphold his end of their bargain. Based on last week's study, what had Jacob promised to do?

_____

_____

Had he fulfilled his promise?

_____

Precisely what does Jacob tell Laban to do to fulfill his part?

_____

_____

In your translation, does the name "Rachel" appear in the verse? In truth it does *not* appear in the Hebrew, which is literally rendered, "please grant my woman." Why is this omission significant?

_____

_____

2. According to verse 22, how does Laban respond to Jacob's demand?

_____

_____

Who is on the guest list?

_____

What is provided for them?

_____

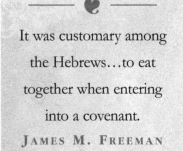

It was customary among the Hebrews...to eat together when entering into a covenant.
JAMES M. FREEMAN

3. The Hebrew word describing this "feast" is derived from the root meaning "drink." Consequently, it would seem they were not only eating food but drinking wine. Similarly, Jesus' first miracle took place at a wedding where wine was served (read John 2:1-3). Drinking wine was not shameful, but being drunk on wine was another matter entirely. Note in each of the passages below what is the outcome of drinking too much wine:

Genesis 9:20-25 _____

Genesis 19:30-36 _____

Proverbs 23:20-21 _____

What does Paul have to say about being inebriated, as found in Ephesians 5:18?

_____

_____

4. In *The Storyteller's Companion to the Bible*, Michael Williams wrote, "The culmination of the feast is always the procession of the bride as she is taken to the tent of the anxious groom." According to Genesis 29:23, at what time of day does this occur?

_____

Why might that be crucial to the story?

_____

_____

What travesty occurs?

_____

_____

Who appears to be responsible?

_____

Does Jacob seem aware of the switch?

_____

5. Now I'm going to turn the tables and ask *you* to jot down any unanswered questions this deceptive scene brings to mind:

a. _____

_____

b. _____

_____

c. _____

_____

6. Given what we know of Laban's nature from previous scenes, can you answer the most compelling question: Why did Laban give *Leah* to Jacob rather than *Rachel*, the woman Jacob loved (and for whom he had labored)? Think of as many possible explanations as you can.

_____

_____

_____

7. Now read back through the following verses leading up to this week's lesson, and note the various clues that foreshadow this wedding night fiasco. I found at least *one* clue in every single verse. See if you can do the same. (Not to worry if some leave you clueless!)

Genesis 29:12 _____

Genesis 29:13 _____

Genesis 29:14 _____

Genesis 29:15 _____

Genesis 29:16 _____

Genesis 29:17 _____

Genesis 29:18 _____

Genesis 29:19 _____

Genesis 29:20 _____

Genesis 29:21 _____

Genesis 29:22 _____

Genesis 29:23 _____

8. One of the ironies of this scene is that Jacob has behaved honorably (for a change *and* for seven years!), yet he is now on the receiving end of deception. Have you ever been in a situation where you were deceived and mistreated even though you had acted honorably and in good faith? Have you…

❑ honored your marriage vows only to have your husband break them?

❑ trusted a friend with a confidence only to have that friend share it with others?

❑ granted a child a privilege only to have that child abuse it?

❑ entered a business deal only to have your partner cheat you?

❑ paid someone to do a job only to have that person not do the work properly?

❑ _____

How did you feel about yourself?

_____

_____

How did you feel about the other person?

_____

_____

How did you feel about God?

_____

_____

What actions did you take?

_____

_____

What wisdom could you gain from Jacob's experience?

_____

_____

Prayer

Merciful Father, when I am mistreated and don't "deserve" it, my first reaction is definitely not to ask you to bless those who have offended me. In fact, I find it difficult ever to ask with sincerity that you bless them. Please help me relinquish any need for payback so that my heart stays clean, because I know I need your grace and mercy just as much as anyone else on earth…

Day Two: Vixen or Victim?

Read Genesis 29:23.

1. At last, after a day-long wedding celebration, Jacob is alone in his tent with his bride. But as Genesis 29:23 tells us, it is not his beloved Rachel who shares his bed; it is her older sister, Leah, thanks to Laban who "gave" or "brought" Leah to Jacob. Laban was nothing if not self-serving. In what ways did Laban stand to benefit from this bridal bait-and-switch?

   _____

   _____

> *This week's verse to remember:*
> "My child, don't ignore it when the LORD disciplines you, and don't be discouraged when he corrects you. For the LORD corrects those he loves, just as a father corrects a child in whom he delights." (Proverbs 3:12, NLT)

2. This deceptive scene echoes one earlier in our study, that of Jacob's pretending to be Esau. Reread Genesis 27:15-16. Then using your imagination and common sense, list below some practical ways Laban might have disguised Leah in order to fool Jacob.

   _____

   _____

   _____

3. Compare the consequences of Laban's deception of Jacob to Jacob's deception of Isaac, considering, among other things, who was affected in each case, how relationships were changed, and how the future was affected. Refer to earlier passages you have read for your answers.

   Jacob's deception of Isaac   Laban's deception of Jacob

   _____   _____

   _____   _____

   _____   _____

   _____   _____

4. We know that even if he wasn't eager to deceive his father, Jacob at least cooperated with his mother, Rebekah, in the plan. But in this scene, we don't hear from Leah, so we cannot be certain *why* she participated with her father in the scheme. Below are several possibilities. Number them in order from *most likely* (1) to *least likely* (5), and then add a few words of explanation for your top two choices.

   _____ Desperate for a husband _____

   _____ In love with Jacob _____

   _____ Anxious for children _____

   _____ Forced by her father _____

   _____ Jealous of her sister _____

   If you've come up with another possible reason, list it below and number it as well:

   _____ _____   _____

> Until we ourselves are injured we do not see how mean and evil it is to injure someone else.
> FRANCES VANDER VELDE

5. Regardless of why Leah participated in the deception, what do the following verses say about our responsibility for our actions?

a. Ezekiel 18:20 _____

b. Matthew 12:36-37 _____

c. Romans 14:11-13 _____

6. How easy it is not to accept responsibility for our behavior. Put a check mark by any of the following thinking patterns you're tempted to engage in.

❏ I can't help it; this is just the way I am.

❏ I'm just like my mother (or father).

❏ My husband (or "my family") won't let me...

❏ I've been this way all my life; it's too late to change now.

❏ We all have shortcomings; mine aren't worse than anyone else's.

❏ I'm not perfect, but God's grace is sufficient.

What is the danger in thinking this way?

_____

_____

In what specific area do you need to take more responsibility for your actions or thoughts or habits?

_____

_____

What specific steps can you take to become more responsible in this area?

_____

_____

Prayer

Gracious Father, I sometimes rationalize away my responsibilities—responsibility for my thoughts, my words, my behavior, my relationship with you. I presume on your grace—and the kindness of others—to overlook my irresponsible behavior. I praise you for your grace and mercy, and I ask that the Holy Spirit guide me in taking control of my thoughts, words, and actions so they come more in line with your will...

Day Three: Just Deserts?

Read Genesis 29:23.

1. At least with old, blind Isaac, we understood how he might have
been deceived. But based on what we've studied so far this week,
how do you explain young Jacob's not recognizing he had the
wrong bride on his wedding night? List below any contributing
factors that might account for Jacob's being so easily deceived.

_____

_____

_____

2. In his book *When Brothers Dwell Together,* Frederick Greenspahn comments, "Laban's
actions have long been recognized as just retribution for Jacob's earlier deceit." Do you
agree that Jacob got what he deserved? Why or why not?

_____

_____

What do the following verses teach us about getting what we deserve?

Job 34:10-11 _____

_____

Jeremiah 17:10_____

_____

3. If we truly got what we deserve for our sins, we would *all* be in trouble. Note below
what each of the following verses says about these questions: What do all of us deserve?
What have we been given? How do we receive this gift?

Romans 3:21-24 _____

_____

Romans 6:22-23 _____

_____

Ephesians 2:1-9 _____

_____

> This was Laban's sin; he
> wronged both Jacob and
> Rachel, whose affections,
> doubtless, were engaged to
> each other, and, if (as
> some say) Leah was herein
> no better than an adulter-
> ess, it was no small wrong
> to her too.
> **MATTHEW HENRY**

4. What encouragement does Psalm 103:8-14 provide for those who fear the Lord?

_____

_____

What three images, or pictures, does the psalmist use in verses 11-13 to help us understand the extent of the Lord's love, forgiveness, and compassion?

_____

_____

Which image is most comforting to you, and why? Consider writing that verse on a note card and putting it in a spot where you will see it daily.

_____

_____

5. Read Psalm 140:4-5, David's cry to God for protection from those who had set traps to ensnare him. It seems a trap was set for Jacob. Have you ever felt as if you walked into a trap of some kind or were set up to fail? Describe (a) the situation, (b) how you felt when you discovered what had happened, and (c) what you learned from the experience.

a. _____

_____

b. _____

_____

c. _____

_____

6. When people are suffering from a painful or seemingly unfair situation, Christians are quick to quote Romans 8:28 as a word of encouragement. Take a moment to jot down that verse here:

_____

_____

One Bible translation, the Contemporary English Version, words this verse a bit differently than most other translations: "We know that God is always at work for the good of everyone who loves him. They are the ones God has chosen for his purpose." Consider both wordings—and look at other translations, if possible—then restate this principle in your own words.

_____

_____

When this verse is misunderstood or misused, it can give people a wrong impression of God, causing anger at God rather than bringing comfort. Have you seen an instance when this happened? If so, describe it.

_____

_____

_____

How could a correct understanding of this verse help us address difficult times?

_____

_____

♥ **7.** Another verse that Christians often quote in such circumstances is 1 Corinthians 10:13. Write out that verse below.

_____

_____

Do you find, as I have, that this verse is often misused? How do people often misstate its promise?

_____

_____

What point *is* Paul making in this verse?

_____

_____

8. For a thorough and practical discussion of what we can do when trouble comes, read Ephesians 6:12-18. What insight does each verse provide?

verse 12 _____

verse 13 _____

verse 14 _____

verse 15 _____

verse 16 _____

verse 17 _____

verse 18 _____

Prayer

All-wise Father, I realize that being your child does not insulate me from sad and unfair and difficult circumstances. When I am engulfed in these trials, help me not to blame you or to turn my back on you but to turn toward you to redeem the circumstances. Help my faith grow deeper through these times so that others may be drawn to you as the source of all goodness, all comfort, and all hope...

WEEK FIVE

Read Genesis 29:24-25.

1. In the middle of this dramatic scene of Jacob's mistaking Leah for his bride, we have verse 24, which seems an intrusive detail at this point. In fact, the Revised Standard Version and the New Revised Standard Version put this verse in parentheses. What fact do we learn?

_____

_____

> **This week's verse to remember:**
> "My child, don't ignore it when the LORD disciplines you, and don't be discouraged when he corrects you. For the LORD corrects those he loves, just as a father corrects a child in whom he delights." (Proverbs 3:12, NLT)

2. Even this detail offers us an insight into the culture and into Laban. It was a wedding custom for the father of the bride to provide her with a personal slave girl. Sharon Pace Jeansonne says, "Laban presumes that Leah will be fertile and gives Zilpah to Leah as a servant—one who could be used as a nursemaid." Yet how does Laban's gift to Leah compare with his gift to Rebekah when she was leaving to marry Isaac (see Genesis 24:59, 61)? What might that tell us about Laban?

_____

_____

3. The title of the Cat Stevens song "Morning Has Broken" (originally a hymn dating from 1931) comes to mind when reading verse 25. Lives were broken and hearts were broken that fateful morning. Most translations include an exclamation point. Does yours? What might that communicate about Jacob's discovery that morning?

_____

_____

To whom does Jacob first turn for an explanation?

_____

What might *that* indicate?

_____

_____

4. In verse 25, Jacob asks three questions in a row without even giving Laban time to respond. Jot down these three brief questions here, and then answer them as Laban *might* have, based on his character and motives.

Jacob: "_____"

Laban: "_____"

Jacob: "_____"

Laban: "_____"

Jacob: "_____"

Laban: "_____"

5. Note that Jacob does not even mention Leah. Why might that be the case?

_____

_____

What do _you_ feel toward Leah at this point in the story? Disgust? Pity? Apathy? Take a moment to put your thoughts about Leah into words

_____

_____

_____

> Jacob's reaction made it utterly clear that there was no place for Leah in his heart.
>
> **GIEN KARSSEN**

6. As with the earlier deception scene in which Jacob was the deceiver and his father was the deceived, we find ourselves asking, "Where is God in all this?" Earlier at Bethel, Jacob had clearly said, "The LORD will be my God" (Genesis 28:21). What evidence do you see of a godly Jacob in this week's verses?

_____

_____

7. When you find yourself in difficult circumstances, which of the following describes how you often _feel?_ You may find yourself checking more than one; in any case, see if you can explain why you chose the one(s) you did.

- ❏ God is too busy or too far away to notice what's happening to me.
- ❏ God is interested in what's happening to me, but he doesn't get directly involved.
- ❏ God is disciplining me for my sins.
- ❏ God is orchestrating the events for my good.
- ❏ God is with me, sustaining me, but he isn't the author of these events.

_____

_____

8. How might the following verses help provide a biblical response to these perceptions of God?

Psalm 145:18-19 _____

_____

Ephesians 2:13-14_____

_____

Romans 8:31-39 _____

_____

Hebrews 12:5-11 _____

_____

Prayer

Patient Father, help me to see your hand more clearly in my life. In the midst of blessings—so many of which I take for granted—I want to praise you more for your faithfulness and generosity. In the midst of trials, I want to feel your comforting presence and to know that you are with me and that you will lead me. I want to trust more fully that you never abandon me, that you never quit loving me, that you always hear my prayers and respond...

Day Five: A Second Wife

Read Genesis 29:26-29.

1. Laban speaks at last, but, goodness…that wasn't what I expected him to say! Study his few words carefully, and then answer the following:

Does Laban express any regret?

_____

Has he mentioned this custom earlier?

_____

Although it was customary, was it a biblical command?

_____

This week's verse to remember:
"My child, don't ignore it when the Lord disciplines you, and don't be discouraged when he corrects you. For the Lord corrects those he loves, just as a father corrects a child in whom he delights." (Proverbs 3:12, NLT)

Is either of his daughters named here?

_____

Does his statement leave room for negotiation?

_____

Based on the above answers, how would you describe Laban's response to Jacob that morning?

_____

_____

❦

The excuse was frivolous….If there had been such a custom, and he had resolved to observe it, he should have told Jacob so.

MATTHEW HENRY

2. We've yet to hear a peep from the two sisters. When we last heard of Rachel, she was preparing to wed Jacob. When we last heard of Leah, she was in her sister's marriage bed. Does it seem to you that Jacob and Laban are taking the women's opinions, feelings, or needs into account? Why might that be the case?

_____

_____

3. The following passages make it clear that what happened on Jacob's wedding night should have been avoided at all costs. Jot down the central message of each verse.

1 Thessalonians 4:3-5 _____

_____

2 Timothy 2:22 _____

_____

Hebrews 13:4 _____

_____

4. In her book *The Women of Genesis,* author Sharon Pace Jeansonne wrote, "Where Laban appears selfish, Jacob appears resigned." Indeed, when we read verse 28, it seems that Jacob agreed to Laban's terms without protest. What reasons might you offer for Jacob being so resigned?

_____

_____

5. Just as Isaac irreversibly blessed the younger son, we have another situation that couldn't be revoked. According to *Nelson's New Illustrated Bible Commentary,* "a public feast in recognition of the union made the marriage between Jacob and Leah official, even though Leah was the wrong woman." Under the circumstances, what could Jacob do to bring any good out of the situation?

_____

_____

6. Read Leviticus 18:18. Uh-oh…sure sounds like what we have going on here! Clyde Francisco, in *The Broadman Bible Commentary,* wrote, "The prohibition probably resulted from the trouble experienced in this family." Without question, Jacob and company are a prime example of how *not* to create a harmonious home life. How does God view such heartless behavior? Proverbs 6:16-19 lists seven things God hates. Note these seven things below and give an example of each—if there is one—from our study of these families.

a. _____

b. _____

c. _____

d. _____

e. _____

f. _____

g. _____

7. Sum up the week's study by stating the various consequences of Laban's switching his daughters:

a. Ethical _____

b. Moral _____

c. Legal _____

d. Sexual _____

e. Emotional _____

f. Spiritual _____

When we sin, we generally don't see all the consequences that ripple out from it. Consider for a moment one sin that is hard for you to overcome, and list below the possible consequences—for you and for others—of your continuing to tolerate that sin.

_____

_____

_____

Prayer

Holy Father, it's easy to see the devastation that was caused by the lying, the trickery, the deceit of this family, but often I am oblivious to the hurt I cause by my sins. I know how it must grieve you. Forgive me for my shortcomings. Make them so distasteful to me that I can finally turn away from them and wholly turn toward you…

After Your Group Discussion…

Restate in your own words the most important principles you learned this week.

How will you respond to these truths?

Video Notes

Insights:

A Heart for God

God's Love Is Powerful Enough to Change Our Hearts

GENESIS 29:30-35

A Heart for God

God's Love Is Powerful Enough to Change Our Hearts

Read Genesis 29:30-35.

Major events:

- Jacob remains married to both women but loves Rachel rather than Leah.

- When God sees that Leah is unloved, he opens her womb and closes Rachel's.

- As Leah bears and names four sons, we see her drawing closer to God.

- Leah discovers an important truth for all of us: God is worthy of our praise.

This week's verse to remember:
"Whom have I in heaven but you? I desire you more
than anything on earth. My health may fail, and my
spirit may grow weak, but God remains the strength of
my heart; he is mine forever." (Psalm 73:25-26, NLT)

Jacob got what he wanted…or did he? Two miserable wives instead of one happy one. And another seven years of labor without pay. He also got a household that was torn asunder with jealousy and strife. Leah and Rachel apparently dwelled in separate tents (Genesis 31:33), but their days and nights spent with Jacob forever tied their sibling relationship into a hard, bitter knot.

Although lovely Rachel seems the innocent party, it's the plight of unloved Leah that tugs at my heart. Imagine waking to find yourself married to someone who did not choose you and does not love you. Who, instead, loves your beautiful, younger sister. Who, in fact, loves her enough to work fourteen *years* for the honor of calling her his wife yet wouldn't willingly work a single *day* for your hand in marriage. *Groan.* Does anyone love Leah? Apparently not her father. Definitely not Jacob. Probably not Rachel.

Only God. But is God's love enough to sustain her—and us? This week in Genesis 29:30-35 we will find our answers.

Day One: Room for Two?

Read Genesis 29:30.

1. One husband, two wives, and two maidservants who later bore Jacob children also—a most unusual means of building a family! *The Interpreter's Dictionary of the Bible* offers several reasons for polygamy: "love and lust, the desire for children, and diplomacy on the part of the nation's rulers. Undoubtedly the need and the desire for sons was the most prominent factor." Those are man's ideas; God's idea was one husband for one wife. Note what the following verses tell us on that subject.

Genesis 2:24 _____

_____

Matthew 19:4-9 _____

_____

> All polygamy came from polytheism—many wives from many gods.
> **GEORGE MATHESON**

2. This verse makes it very clear where Jacob's affections rest. The King James Version states, "He loved also Rachel more than Leah," and the New English Bible says, "He loved her rather than Leah." Big difference there! How does your translation compare Jacob's feelings for Rachel to his feelings for Leah? Does your version include "also" or "more than" or "rather than"…or something else altogether?

_____

What indications do we have at this point in the story regarding Jacob's true feelings for Leah, positive or negative?

_____

3. Verse 30 concludes with this simple statement: "He worked for Laban another seven years." What would have been *different* about those seven years compared to the first seven? Think through all the dimensions—practical, emotional, spiritual—that might have been part of Jacob's experience throughout that *second* term of unpaid labor.

_____

_____

_____

_____

4. Although Laban may have intended those seven additional years to benefit him alone, God can use such times in our lives to test and refine our faith. What do the following verses teach us about the value of trials?

James 1:2-4_____

_____

James 1:12 _____

_____

1 Peter 1:6-7_____

_____

1 Peter 4:12-13 _____

_____

5. And what Jacob may have seen only as Laban's greed and deceit, God may have seen as an opportunity to discipline the chosen Jacob (something that many of us have longed to see!). What do the following passages have to say about the value of discipline and especially the value of God's discipline?

Job 5:17 _____

Proverbs 3:11-12 _____

Proverbs 10:17 _____

Proverbs 12:1-2 _____

Proverbs 15:32 _____
What warnings do these verses give about those who reject discipline?

_____

_____

And what positive outcome is suggested if we accept God's discipline?

_____

_____

6. According to the dictionary, discipline can in part be defined as "the rigor or training effect of experience, adversity, etc." Describe a time when you felt that God was disciplining you through an experience of adversity.

What was the discipline?

_____

_____

What changes did it bring about?

_____

_____

How might your life have been different if God had not disciplined you?

_____

_____

How might other lives have been affected if you had not been disciplined?

_____

_____

Can you now say, as Paul did, that the discipline was to your benefit and God's glory?

_____

_____

Prayer

Gracious Father, you know I don't like to be disciplined. My pride is wounded, and often something I have "idolized" is wrested out of my hands. Even though I don't like it, I understand that your discipline shows you haven't given up on me and that you are trying to form me more into the image of your Son. Help me to accept your discipline with humility and understanding so that you
will be glorified…

Day Two: Precious in God's Sight

Read Genesis 29:31.

1. Jacob is not the only one whom God was watching over. Write out the first phrase found in verse 31:

_____

_____

_____

It's easy to get so caught up in the description of Leah's loveless state that we miss the important opening words, "When the LORD saw..." Restate and personalize each of the following verses to encourage *you* to remember that God sees you, even when you (like Leah) fear no one is paying attention to you at all.

2 Chronicles 16:9a _____

_____

Job 34:21 _____

_____

Psalm 33:13-15 _____

_____

2. With those promises fresh in your mind, why not ask the Lord to "keep his eye on you" concerning a particular situation you are dealing with right now. Write it below as a prayer request and note the date. Later you can rejoice when you see your prayer has been answered. No need to share this with your small group if you're not comfortable doing so; this is between you and the One who sees.

Today's Date: _____ Date God Answered: _____

Dear Lord, please keep your eye on me as I...

_____

_____

_____

3. These very words—"When the Lord saw"—appear in the NIV translation only once in the New Testament, as part of a story involving the Lord Jesus and another woman in distress. Read Luke 7:11-17 and then note what you've learned from this passage.

What do we know about the woman in this story?

_____

How does Jesus initially respond to her—physically, emotionally, then verbally?

_____

_____

What actions does Jesus take to remedy the dire situation?

_____

_____

To whom do the people give credit?

_____

How does this story build *your* faith in a Lord who "sees" our sorrow and takes action?

_____

_____

_____

> God cared for these women, not for what they could do for His nation, but because they were individuals who had special needs.
>
> **JULIA STATON**

♥ **4.** According to *Nelson's New Illustrated Bible Commentary,* "As near as we can tell, many cultures in the ancient world viewed women as little more than property. Furthermore, the men who recorded the literature of those times tended to overlook the presence and significance of their female counterparts. By contrast, the Bible not only includes women but also tells about their leadership, contributions, and feelings, and not just their sins and failures." In addition to Leah and the widow just mentioned, we find many examples in the Bible of God's seeing the plight of women—and responding. Let's look at three of them. How does God intervene in each of these women's lives?

	The woman	The problem	God's intervention
1 Samuel 1:1-20	_____	_____	_____
Mark 5:24-34	_____	_____	_____
John 4:3-29	_____	_____	_____

5. While the NIV translates the Hebrew as "Leah was not loved," others render it "Leah was hated" (RSV) and "Leah was despised" (AMP). Ouch! Take a moment to compare various translations of that phrase with others in your small group. To be "unloved" (NASB) suggests a passive, unemotional detachment; to be "hated" (KJV) sounds more aggressive and intentional.

Which of these phrases best describes Jacob's treatment of Leah?

_____

Why do you say that?

_____

_____

How might he have demonstrated these feelings toward her on a day-to-day basis?

_____

_____

6. As for Leah, we can imagine her calling out to God in her prayers, beseeching his favor, just as David often did many centuries later. Read the following verses from Psalms and note what comfort or wisdom you find in each. Choose the verse or verses that best apply to your situation mentioned in question 2, and consider making it a part of your store of memory verses.

Psalm 10:14 _____

Psalm 25:19-21 _____

Psalm 86:17 _____

Psalm 109:25-27 _____

7. The Lord not only *sees* that Leah is unloved, he *saves* her from despair. According to verse 31, what does God do for Leah?

_____

By contrast, what is Rachel's situation?

_____

Rachel's condition was not unique among the matriarchs of the Old Testament or among the godly mothers of the New Testament, according to the following verses.

	Woman's name	Her affliction	God's response
Genesis 11:30; 17:19	_____	_____	_____
Genesis 25:21	_____	_____	_____
Luke 1:7, 24-25	_____	_____	_____

8. Based on all these examples of what God has done for women in the Bible, how would you describe his ability and willingness to help you in your present circumstances?

_____

_____

_____

Prayer

Merciful Father, I am overwhelmed by the thought that you see my every move and hear my every cry. I bring to you my burdens, and I take shelter in your arms. And for every blessing you put in my life and every time you rescue me, I praise you and give you all the glory. Thank you that I am not less important to you just because I am a woman...

Loved by God

Day Three: Blessings for the Humble

Read Genesis 29:32.

1. Leah's womb is not only opened; it is filled. Unto Leah a child is born. Note your answers to the following questions based on this verse.

Is it a boy or girl? _____

Why does that matter? _____

Who names this child? _____

What is that name? _____

Whom does Leah credit for her son? _____

What outcome does Leah hope for? _____

2. According to the Law of Moses, which reflects many long-standing principles, this child from Leah is to be favored over any child from Rachel. Let's look at Deuteronomy 21:15-17 and find out why.

What situation does the Law address here that suits the Leah-Rachel fiasco to a *T*?

_____

_____

Which son is to receive the greater honor in the father's will?

_____

In what specific way is the father to honor this son?

_____

_____

Why do you think this law was put into place?

_____

_____

3. "Reuben" literally means "Look, a son!" What do the following verses from Psalms tell us about the value of children to a father?

Psalm 45:16-17 _____

Psalm 127:3-5 _____

Psalm 128:3-4 _____

Do we find any evidence in our story that Jacob responded to the birth of this first son or to the woman who bore him?

_____

> *This week's verse to remember:*
> "Whom have I in heaven but you? I desire you more than anything on earth. My health may fail, and my spirit may grow weak, but God remains the strength of my heart; he is mine forever." (Psalm 73:25-26, NLT)

> Barrenness was a shame and a reproach in Israel; it was interpreted as divine punishment or at least a sign of divine displeasure.
>
> PHYLLIS A. BIRD

4. It is clear that Jacob does *not* favor Leah; it is equally clear that God *does*. Examine closely 1 Corinthians 1:27-29 and see if the truth we find there fits our unloved Leah.

How has Leah been "foolish"?

_____

_____

In what way is Leah viewed as "weak"?

_____

_____

How might the word "lowly" suit Leah?

_____

_____

Who "despises" Leah?

_____

What "things" might Leah "not" possess?

_____

_____

To what end does God use all of the above?

_____

_____

5. Of the many words that might describe Leah, *humble* is surely one of the best. Using your dictionary, give two or three definitions for *humble* that apply to Leah.

_____

_____

And in what way might each of the following verses describe Leah?

Isaiah 66:2 _____

Ephesians 4:1-3_____

James 4:10 _____

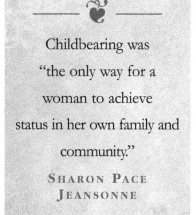

Childbearing was "the only way for a woman to achieve status in her own family and community."

SHARON PACE JEANSONNE

6. Humility is not our favorite virtue to pursue. As a friend said, "I'd be willing to be humble if everybody else would go first." What do the following verses teach us about God's view of humility?

Psalm 25:9-10 _____

Proverbs 22:4 _____

1 Peter 5:6-7 _____

7. How would you rate your humility level? Put an "X" to show where you would place yourself on the scale below.

Pride   Humility

1   2   3   4   5

In what specific ways could you work on moving away from pride and toward humility?

_____

_____

_____

Prayer

Heavenly Father, just like Leah, I don't always receive the answers to my prayers that I want. But I pray that you will help me see the answers you send and that I will humbly receive them as what is best for me. Help me see the ways in which my pride hinders me from learning what you would teach me. Help me be able to say, as Mary did, "I am the Lord's servant, and I am willing to accept whatever he wants" (Luke 1:38, NLT)…

Day Four: The One Who Always Hears

Read Genesis 29:33-34.

1. One child would have been sufficient for Leah to have considered herself blessed. Sarah in the Old Testament and Elizabeth in the New Testament each gave birth to just one son. But fertile Leah gives birth again.

   Was this second child a son or daughter? _____

   To whom does Leah give credit? _____

   With the first child, she said God *saw* her misery. What does Leah say this time?

   _____

   Again, who named the babe? _____

   And what is the child's name? _____

> **This week's verse to remember:**
> "Whom have I in heaven but you? I desire you more than anything on earth. My health may fail, and my spirit may grow weak, but God remains the strength of my heart; he is mine forever." (Psalm 73:25-26, NLT)

2. It is comforting to know that our God watches over us and even more encouraging to realize he *hears* and *listens.* Restate in your own words the assurance you find in the following verses from Psalms.

   Psalm 10:17-18 _____

   _____

   Psalm 22:23-24 _____

   _____

   Psalm 34:17-18 _____

   _____

3. The name "Simeon" means "listening." Not only was God listening to Leah, even as he is listening now to us, but God also calls us to listen to *him.* Spend a few moments in the New Testament and note what Jesus asks us to do.

   Luke 6:46-49 _____

   Luke 9:35 _____

   John 10:27-28 _____

4. In these verses we also learn that a third son is born to Leah and Jacob. At the previous birth, Leah mentions God but not Jacob. What do we see at *this* birth?

   _____

   What does Leah hope will happen this time?

   _____

   And why is she convinced it will?

   _____

> The names Leah gave her children testified to the miraculous faith God had planted in her heart.
>
> HERBERT LOCKYER

Who named this third baby?

_____

And what is the child's name, which in Hebrew means "to cleave"?

_____

5. The sons of Levi were very important to the nation of Israel. Read Deuteronomy 10:8 and 21:5. What were the duties of the Levites?

_____

_____

Perhaps the most famous of the Levites is introduced in Exodus 2:1-10. What's the name of this baby, born to a Levite couple?

_____

According to Hebrews 11:24-26, what legacy of faith did this famous Levite leave?

_____

_____

6. God has watched, God has listened, God has blessed Leah's womb three times, the number of holiness. Does Jacob seem to be paying attention?

_____

What explanation would you offer?

_____

_____

_____

7. Have you ever been in a situation that sounds similar to Leah's—thinking you can win or earn someone's appreciation or love but seeing no results? Might that person be a man, a husband, a parent, an in-law, a sibling, a child? Based on what you have learned from Leah's life thus far, what words of wisdom would you offer to a person stuck in this situation?

_____

_____

_____

Day Five: Praise the Lord

Read Genesis 29:35.

1. When Leah gives birth to her fourth child, something extraordinary happens to her spiritually.

   What does Leah say about Jacob? _____

   What does she say about God? _____

   _____

   _____

   How would you describe her attitude? _____

   Who names this child? _____

   And what name is he given? _____

> *This week's verse to remember:*
>
> "Whom have I in heaven but you? I desire you more than anything on earth. My health may fail, and my spirit may grow weak, but God remains the strength of my heart; he is mine forever." (Psalm 73:25-26, NLT)

2. "Judah" means "praise," a jubilant expression of Leah's heart toward God. In the NIV translation, this is the first time in Scripture we see the exact phrase "Praise the Lord"…but it is not the last. (In fact, the word "praise" and its variant forms appear 420 times in the NIV!) There are innumerable reasons to praise God. Note below just a few of them as found in the following verses.

   Psalm 68:19 _____

   Psalm 86:5-10 _____

   Psalm 93:1-2 _____

   Jeremiah 10:6 _____

   2 Corinthians 1:3-4 _____

   Revelation 4:11 _____

3. Knowing all the heartache that has come before this moment, describe what *you* see happening in Leah's life, emotionally and spiritually, with the birth of this fourth child and why this might be the case.

   _____

   _____

4. Have you had a similar epiphany in your spiritual journey, an instance when you discovered some life-changing truth? Leah came to a point of desperation before she came to a place of praise. Is that how it was for you? Take a moment to put your experience into words.

   _____

   _____

Did you, like Leah, "praise the Lord" at the time it happened?

_____

How would you praise God now for the changes that discovery has brought to your life?

_____

_____

_____

_____

> "Three people never start-ed life together against greater odds, but God was in it with them." In fact, "God is the main Character in the drama."
> **EUGENIA PRICE**

5. When Judah is grown, his father, Jacob, speaks a prophetic word over this son. Read Genesis 49:8-10 and note all that is to come in Judah's life.

_____

_____

What elements of Judah's blessing do you find in Isaac's blessing of Jacob (Genesis 27:28-29)?

_____

_____

6. In truth, it is not only Judah himself who will rule nor simply the tribe that bears his name. Centuries later a ruler will come from the lineage of Judah who will reign for all time. Note what the following verses teach us about this Lion of Judah.

Matthew 1:1-2 _____

Matthew 2:6 _____

Hebrews 7:14 _____

7. In her book *Caught in a Higher Love,* author Carolyn Baker writes: "On the one hand Leah's story is one of heartbreak. On the other it is a story of triumph." The heartbreak is obvious. How is Leah's story one of triumph?

_____

_____

_____

8. Although the story of Leah, Rachel, and Jacob is far from over, I've chosen to end our study here with good purpose: The focus rests on God and on the coming of his Son, Jesus. Just as Leah realized that the Lord was her only hope, her true source of joy, and worthy of her praise, so must we come to the same conclusion if we are to be truly at peace with ourselves and with God. Though David wrote Psalm 62:5, the words sound like something Leah might have whispered while she cradled the baby Judah in her arms. Write out Psalm 62:5 here:

_____

_____

Now put these same thoughts in your own words, personalizing them by applying them to your own life and your own desire to trust in the promises of God and experience his blessings. Treat it as the Amplified Bible would—expanding the words and phrases to make the verse more specific and applicable to you.

_____

_____

_____

9. I said at the beginning of this study that I had a three-point mission: (1) for you to know how much God loves you; (2) for you to realize that you can trust his promises—as long as you don't hold him to your timing; and (3) for you to experience his blessings—as long as you are willing to look at a new definition of "blessing." As we close this series, let's reflect on these three goals.

    How has your awareness of how much God loves you grown?

    _____

    _____

    _____

    What verse or biblical example helped reinforce your awareness of God's love for you?

    _____

    _____

    In what ways has your trust in his promises increased?

    _____

    _____

    Which of his promises has made the greatest impact on you?

    _____

    _____

    What blessings have you become more aware of in your life?

    _____

    _____

    How do you want to respond to God in light of what you've learned?

    _____

    _____

    _____

Prayer

Loving Father, thank you for providing your written Word so I can read and study your heart-changing message throughout my life. Open my eyes to see who you are and what you have done for me. Sharpen my hearing to perceive the leading of your Spirit. Soften my heart to respond to your will for my life. I pray that I will draw closer to you every day and will grow into the likeness of your Son...

Loved by God

Loved by God

Closing thoughts from Liz...

Dear one, this time with you—on video and on paper—has been an absolute delight! As I prepared the seven messages and crafted the many questions you've answered, I prayed for you, knowing we had much ground to cover together as we explored the timeless truths of God's Word. Bless you for being willing to make the journey!

Now I'll continue to pray that the lessons you've learned here will take root and blossom in your life...that your trust in him will grow deeper and your awareness of his many blessings will increase. Truly, my friend, you are loved by God!

Liz Curtis Higgs

P.S. Isn't it wonderful that Christian sisters never need to say a last good-bye? Instead, I'll leave you with a long-distance hug and these encouraging words from 2 Thessalonians 2:16-17:

**May our Lord Jesus Christ himself and God our Father,
who loved us and by his grace gave us eternal encouragement and good hope,
encourage your hearts and strengthen you in every good deed and word.**

After Your Group Discussion...

Restate in your own words the most important principles you learned this last week of the study.

How will you respond to these truths?

Video Notes

Insights:

Fifteen Recommended Study Resources for

Loved by God

A Bible Study with Liz Curtis Higgs

Alter, Robert. *Genesis: Translation and Commentary.* New York: W.W. Norton & Company, 1996.

Baker, Carolyn Nabors. *Caught in a Higher Love.* Nashville: Broadman & Holman Publishers, 1998.

Elliott, Ralph H. *The Message of Genesis.* St. Louis: Abbot Books, 1962.

Francisco, Clyde. *Genesis: The Broadman Bible Commentary.* Vol. 1. Nashville: Broadman Press, 1969.

Freeman, James M. *Manners and Customs of the Bible.* New Kensington, Pa.: Whitaker House, 1996.

Hartley, John E. *New International Biblical Commentary: Genesis.* Peabody, Mass.: Hendrickson Publishers, 2000.

Henry, Matthew. *Matthew Henry's Commentary on the Whole Bible.* Vol. 1. 1706. Reprint, Peabody, Mass: Hendrickson Publishers, 1991.

Jeansonne, Sharon Pace. *The Women of Genesis.* Minneapolis: Fortress Press, 1990.

Kam, Rose Salberg. *Their Stories, Our Stories.* New York: Continuum Publishing Company, 1995.

Kidner, Derek. *Genesis: An Introduction and Commentary.* Downers Grove, Ill.: Tyndale Press, 1967.

Owens, Virginia Stem. *Daughters of Eve.* Colorado Springs: NavPress, 1995.

Raver, Miki. *Listen to Her Voice: Women of the Hebrew Bible.* San Francisco: Chronicle Books, 1998.

von Rad, Gerhard. *Genesis: A Commentary.* Philadelphia: Westminster Press, 1972.

Wiersbe, Warren W. *Be Authentic.* Colorado Springs: Chariot Victor Publishing, 1997.

Williams, Michael E., ed. *The Storyteller's Companion to the Bible.* Vol. 4, *Old Testament Women.* Nashville: Abingdon Press, 1993.

Notes

Welcome to the Family!

1. "God often outdoes...," Matthew Henry, *Matthew Henry's Commentary on the Whole Bible*, vol. 1 (1706; reprint, Peabody, Mass: Hendrickson Publishers, 1991), 124.

2. "Isaac wasn't praying selfishly...," Warren W. Wiersbe, *Be Authentic* (Colorado Springs: Chariot Victor Publishing, 1997), 12.

Week One: Sibling Rivalry

1. "They personified two ways...," Gerhard von Rad, *Genesis: A Commentary* (Philadelphia: Westminster Press, 1972), 265-66.

2. "applied to certain advantages...," H. L. Willmington, *Willmington's Guide to the Bible* (Wheaton, Ill.: Tyndale House, 1981), commentary on Genesis 25:27-34.

3. "He was defrauded...," Ralph H. Elliott, *The Message of Genesis* (St. Louis, Mo.: Abbot Books, 1962), 162.

4. "Blessing is the transmission...," von Rad, *Genesis*, 277.

5. "She operates behind the scenes...," Christiana de Groot, *The IVP Women's Bible Commentary (Genesis)* (Downers Grove, Ill.: InterVarsity Press, 2002), 17.

6. "The deceiver...," Meredith G. Kline, *Genesis*, of *The New Bible Commentary*, rev. ed. (Grand Rapids: Wm. B. Eerdsman Publishing, 1970), 102.

7. "An abundant measure...," James G. Murphy, *Barnes' Notes: Genesis* (1873; reprint, Grand Rapids: Baker Books, 1998), 382.

Week Two: Running from God

1. "It is almost as impossible...," Clyde Francisco, *The Broadman Bible Commentary: Genesis*, vol. 1 (Nashville: Broadman Press, 1969), 206.

2. "The tree was shaken...," Francisco, *The Broadman Bible Commentary: Genesis*, 207.

3. "Esau's tears were not...," Wiersbe, *Be Authentic*, 30.

4. "The paternal benediction...," Murphy, *Barnes' Notes: Genesis*, 383.

5. "The history of Edom...," Murphy, *Barnes' Notes: Genesis*, 383.

6. "Her tactics are questionable...," de Groot, *The IVP Women's Bible Commentary: Genesis*, 18.

7. "The Old Testament term...," Derek Kidner, *Genesis: An Introduction and Commentary* (Downers Grove, Ill.: Tyndale Press, 1967), 158.

8. "God left [Rebekah]...," Henry, *Matthew Henry's Commentary on the Whole Bible*, 131.

9. "Esau's response to this news...," Wiersbe, *Be Authentic*, 31.

Week Three: A Dream Come True

1. "There could not have been ...," Francisco, *The Broadman Bible Commentary*, 210.

2. "This is the greatest promise...," John E. Hartley, *New International Biblical Commentary: Genesis* (Peabody, Mass.: Hendrickson Publishers, 2000), 256.

3. "When God appears...," Trent C. Butler, ed., *Holman Bible Dictionary* (Nashville: Holman Bible Publishers, 1991), see "religious fear: fear of God."

4. "In pagan belief a site...," Hartley, *New International Biblical Commentary: Genesis*, 255-56.

5. "The biblical concept of naming...," Butler, *Holman Bible Dictionary*, see "naming."

6. "By making such a contribution...," Hartley, *New International Biblical Commentary: Genesis*, 258.

Week Four: Blinded by Love

1. "He tries to rid the scene...," Rose Salberg Kam, *Their Stories, Our Stories* (New York: Continuum Publishing, 1995), 62.

2. "In rolling the stone...," Francisco, *The Broadman Bible Commentary*, 212.

3. "Tradition has it...," Barbara L. Thaw Ronson, *The Women of the Torah* (Jerusalem: Jason Aronson, Inc., 1999), 120.

4. "Perhaps Rachel is...," Alice Ogden Bellis, *Helpmates, Harlots, and Heroes* (Louisville, Ky.: Westminster/John Knox Press, 1994), 85.

5. "Custom regards the father...," James M. Freeman, *Manners and Customs of the Bible* (New Kensington, Pa.: Whitaker House, 1996), 37.

6. "No man who loved...," Francisco, *The Broadman Bible Commentary*, 213.

Week Five: A Deceiver Deceived

1. "It was customary...," Freeman, *Manners and Customs of the Bible*, 34.
2. "The culmination of the feast...," Michael E. Williams, ed., *The Storyteller's Companion to the Bible* (Nashville, Abingdon Press, 1991), 146.
3. "Until we ourselves are injured...," Frances Vander Velde, *Women of the Bible* (Grand Rapids: Kregel Publications, 1985), 61.
4. "Laban's actions have long...," Frederick E, Greenspahn, *When Brothers Dwell Together* (Oxford: Oxford University Press, 1994), 128.
5. "This was Laban's sin...," Henry, *Matthew Henry's Commentary on the Whole Bible*, 141.
6. "Laban presumes that...," Sharon Pace Jeansonne, *The Women of Genesis* (Minneapolis: Fortress Press, 1990), 73.
7. "Jacob's reaction...," Gien Karssen, *Her Name Is Woman*, book 2 (Colorado Springs: NavPress, 1977), 49.
8. "The excuse was frivolous...," Henry, *Matthew Henry's Commentary on the Whole Bible*, 141.
9. "Where Laban appears selfish...," Jeansonne, *The Women of Genesis*, 73-74.
10. "a public feast...," Earl D. Radmacher, gen. ed., *Nelson's New Illustrated Bible Commentary* (Nashville: T. Nelson Publishers, 1999), commentary on Genesis 29:23.
11. "This prohibition probably...," Francisco, *The Broadman Bible Commentary*, 214.

Week 6: A Heart for God

1. "love and lust...," George Arthur Buttrick, ed., *The Interpreter's Dictionary of the Bible*, vol. 3 (New York: Abingdon Press, 1962), 280.
2. "All polygamy...," George Matheson, *The Representative Women of the Bible* (London: Hodder and Stoughton, 1908), 120.
3. "As near as we can tell...," Radmacher, *Nelson's New Illustrated Bible Commentary*, commentary at Genesis 29:30, 31, entitled "Women in the Ancient World."
4. "God cared for these women...," Julia Staton, *What the Bible Says About Women* (Joplin, Mo.: College Press Publishing, 1980), 54-55.
5. "Barrenness was a shame...," Phyllis A. Bird, *Missing Persons and Mistaken Identities* (Minneapolis: Augsburg Fortress Press, 1997), 35.
6. "the only way for a woman...," Jeansonne, *The Women of Genesis*, 75.
7. "The names Leah gave...," Herbert Lockyer, *All the Women of the Bible* (Grand Rapids: Zondervan, 1967), 82.
8. "Three people never started...," "God is the main Character...," Eugenia Price, *God Speaks to Women Today* (Grand Rapids: Zondervan Publishing, 1964), 69, 64.
9. "On the one hand...," Carolyn Nabors Baker, *Caught in a Higher Love* (Nashville: Broadman & Holman Publishers, 1998), 70.

CPSIA information can be obtained
at www.ICGtesting.com
Printed in the USA
BVHW01s1008070818
523241BV00010B/8/P